Core Skills
for
Family Ministry

Inside illustrations: Rebecca J Hall

Published by
The Bible Reading Fellowship
15 The Chambers, Vineyard
Abingdon, OX14 3FE
United Kingdom
Tel: +44 (0)1865 319700
Email: enquiries@brf.org.uk
Website: www.brf.org.uk
BRF is a Registered Charity

ISBN 978 0 85746 431 6
First published 2015
10 9 8 7 6 5 4 3 2 1 0

Acknowledgements
Unless otherwise stated, scripture quotations are taken from The Holy Bible, New International Version (Anglicised edition) copyright © 1973, 1978, 1984, 2011 by Biblica (formerly International Bible Society). Used by permission of Hodder & Stoughton Publishers, an Hachette UK company. All rights reserved. 'NIV' is a registered trade mark of Biblica (formerly International Bible Society). UK trademark number 1448790.

Scripture quotations taken from the Holy Bible, English Standard Version, published by HarperCollins Publishers, © 2001 Crossway Bibles, a division of Good News Publishers. Used by permission. All rights reserved.

Scripture taken from *The Message*. Copyright © 1993, 1994, 1995, 1996, 2000, 2001, 2002. Used by permission of NavPress Publishing Group.

Every effort has been made to trace and contact copyright owners for material used in this resource. We apologise for any inadvertent omissions or errors, and would ask those concerned to contact us so that full acknowledgement can be made in the future.

A catalogue record for this book is available from the British Library

Printed by Gutenberg Press, Tarxien, Malta

Developing key skills for church-based family ministry

Core Skills for Family Ministry

THE CONSULTATIVE GROUP ON MINISTRY AMONG CHILDREN

Important information

Photocopying permission

The right to photocopy material in *Core Skills for Family Ministry* is granted for the pages that contain the photocopying clause: 'Reproduced with permission from *Core Skills for Family Ministry* by CGMC (Barnabas for Children, 2015) www.barnabasinchurches.org.uk', so long as reproduction is for use in a teaching situation by the original purchaser. The right to photocopy material is not granted for anyone other than the original purchaser without written permission from BRF.

The Copyright Licensing Agency (CLA)

If you are resident in the UK and you have a photocopying licence with the Copyright Licensing Agency (CLA) please check the terms of your licence. If your photocopying request falls within the terms of your licence, you may proceed without seeking further permission. If your request exceeds the terms of your CLA licence, please contact the CLA directly with your request. Copyright Licensing Agency, Saffron House, 6–10 Kirby Street, London EC1N 8TS, UK, Tel: 020 7400 3100, email cla@cla.co.uk; web www.cla.co.uk. The CLA will provide photocopying authorisation and royalty fee information on behalf of BRF.

BRF is Registered Charity No. 233280

Download templates and handout sheets at www.barnabasinchurches.org.uk/9780857464316

Contents

Acknowledgements

CGMC wishes to thank all those involved with the project, either with the writing or with the field-testing of material, and is grateful for their ideas, inspiration and hard work.

Particular thanks go to the writing group:

Gail Adcock
Mo Baldwin
Jane Butcher
Valerie Mylechreest
Martyn Payne
Sarah Smart
Ian White

Introduction

All people are made in the image of God, loved unconditionally and affirmed in the life and ministry of Jesus. This is reflected in the Christian community where:

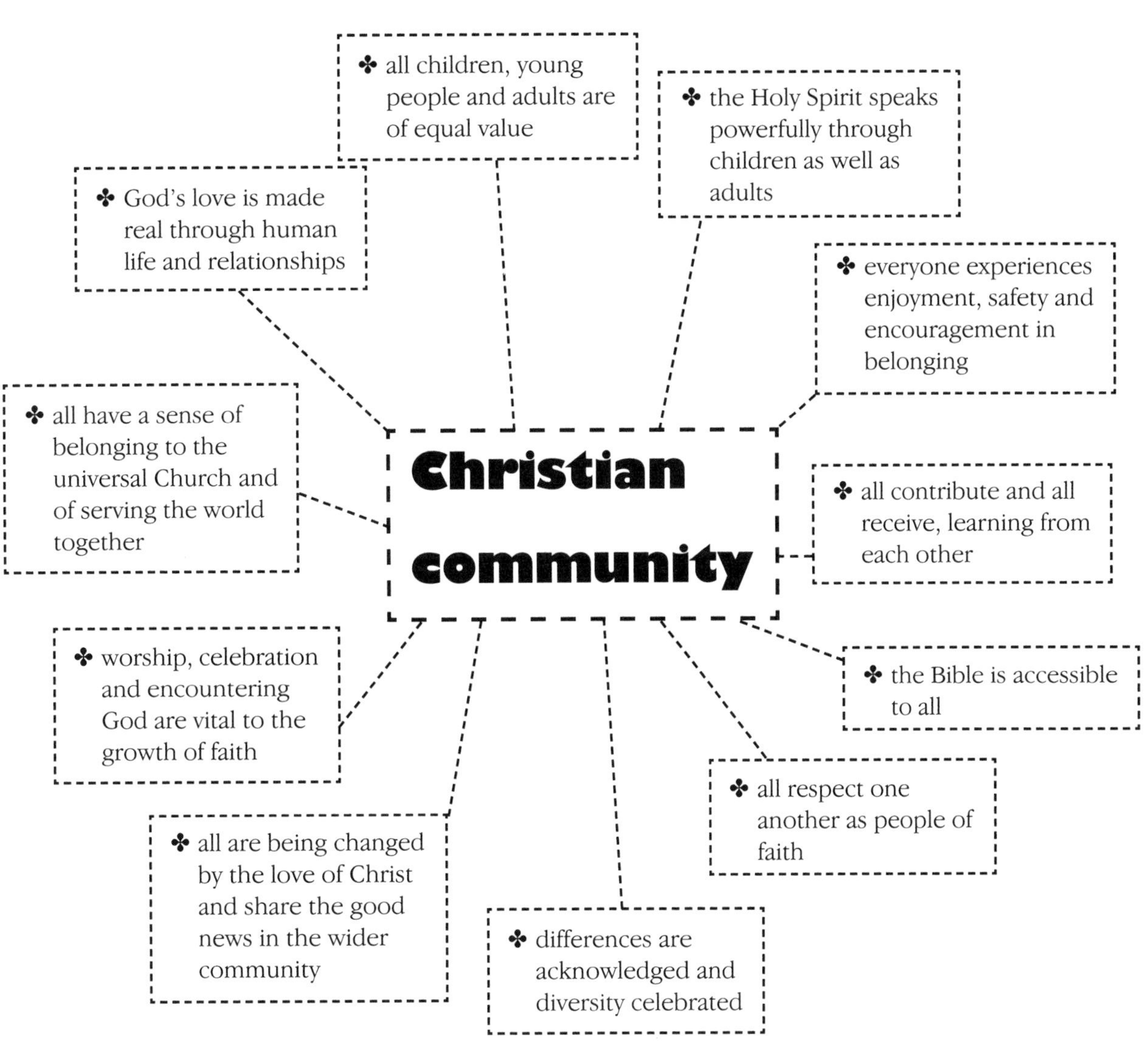

The current context of family

The UN has sought to highlight the place of family in society and the opportunities and challenges it faces. Their statements on family suggest that owing to rapid socio-economic and demographic transformations, families find it increasingly difficult to fulfil their numerous responsibilities. Many struggle to overcome poverty and adequately provide for younger and older family members. It is also harder for them to reconcile work and family commitments and maintain the intergenerational bonds that sustained them in the past. The impact of low incomes, relationship breakdown, employment pressure and other life experiences is felt by all members of the family.

Defining 'family' can be difficult these days. In this resource we are using the term 'family' to include and group people who consider themselves family, whether biological, legal or any other form, structure or context in which a family exists. This includes children and young people of all ages.

Adults' experience of family life will be varied and issues may arise for some in your group. It is not your responsibility to deal with or address these. However, it is beneficial to be aware of external support available that can be signposted to should it be needed. It would be valuable to find out about local services before the start of the course.

Safeguarding and Child Protection

Core Skills for Family Ministry does not include Child Protection training. Most denominations or organisations in Britain and Ireland have their own policies, procedures and training, to which all participants should look. You should also be aware of relevant support available in your area or organisation, should the need arise.

We recommend that the information sheet on the following page is completed by all participants before starting the course. A copy of this sheet can then be included in their portfolio.

Safeguarding and child protection

Title of your denomination's policy document:

What do you do if you have an issue relating to child protection?

Who is the person in your church who deals with child protection issues?

What training in child protection have you had?

If none, when is the next available training?

When is the next review of your local child protection procedures?

At-a-glance summary of aims and learning outcomes

Introductory session

Aim

- ✤ To provide a basic introduction to working with families in a church context
- ✤ To begin to engage participants in the content of the course

Learning outcomes

- ✤ To share hopes and fears about working with families
- ✤ To reflect critically on a variety of strategies for developing relationships with families
- ✤ To explore issues around families, theology and culture
- ✤ To consider how to approach a session with families
- ✤ To acknowledge and reflect on our personal experiences of family, and to recognise how this might impact on our approach to family ministry

Core Session One: Biblical, historical and contemporary understanding of family

Aim

- ✤ To introduce participants to biblical and contemporary understandings and meanings of family.

Learning outcomes

- ✤ To gain insight into the biblical and historical understandings surrounding family
- ✤ To reflect on the differences and similarities between historical and contemporary situations
- ✤ To reflect on the structure of your own family, and of those around them

Core Session Two: Family ministry today

Aim

- ✤ To recognise the importance of relevant work with families in a rapidly changing world

Learning outcomes

- ✤ To explore opportunities for families and churches to engage with each other
- ✤ To recognise the contemporary context of family life

Core Session Three: Seasons of family life

Aim

- ✤ To reflect on and understand that there are different seasons of life for families, applying this understanding to interaction with families and exploring ways the church can affirm and support them

Learning outcomes

- ✤ To recognise the role of the church in the various seasons of family life
- ✤ To reflect on the occasions when families may celebrate and commemorate significant milestones experienced in their lives
- ✤ To appreciate the importance of managing these seasons well
- ✤ To be equipped and gain tools to support and resource families during these seasons of life

Core Session Four: Role of family relationships

Aim

- ✤ To understand the role of relationships within families and between families and their community, including the church
- ✤ To explore how the church might offer additional support where relationships are missing or dysfunctional

Learning outcomes

- ✤ To reflect on traditional relationships and consider the implications for families if some of these relationships are missing or distorted (for example, mother/child, father/child, husband/wife, grandparent/child, neighbours, siblings, family/school, family/GP, family/vicar)
- ✤ To plan ways to develop and strengthen relationships with families
- ✤ To explore how the church might offer specific support to families to help alleviate the impact of a missing or distorted relationship

Core Session Five: Family well-being and wholeness

Aim

- ✤ To understand what subjective well-being is for children and young people
- ✤ To understand which aspects of life have the greatest influence on children and young people's well-being
- ✤ To consider how the church can listen to and involve families, children and young people to improve and support the collective well-being of families

Learning outcomes

- ✤ To gain a clearer understanding of the influence and impact of well-being on the life of families
- ✤ To develop thinking and inform future practice to ensure full participation by families in the life of the church

Core Session Six: Faith in families

Aim

- ✤ To reflect on and understand the challenges and limitations that families may face in living out faith in the home
- ✤ To consider the ways in which the church can encourage, support and resource families in practical ways, and the resources available to do so

Learning outcomes

- ✤ To recognise the role of the church in supporting families to live out faith in the home in a way that is appropriate and accessible for families
- ✤ To recognise the different factors to be taken into account when working with families, such as age, experience, time and finance
- ✤ To equip leaders to help families create faith-filled homes

Using Core Skills for Family Ministry

This resource is planned for ease of use in a variety of ways. As the material has been written from a number of ecumenical settings, it is hoped that it will be delivered ecumenically wherever possible.

If you would like to know where your nearest Core Skills course is happening:

- ✤ visit the CGMC website www.cgmcontheweb.com or contact CGMC via the website
- ✤ ask your denominational or organisational office

The six sessions in *Core Skills for Family Ministry* are designed as stand-alone modules, covering specific areas related to family ministry. It is expected that an individual or group will select an initial module appropriate to their needs and potentially move on to cover the remaining modules at a future date.

Each session is designed to take two hours. This timespan will be achieved by selecting from the material available. Each session could be extended to cover a whole day by using more of the material, adding some from the website and slowing the pace to allow more discussion, exploration and activity.

The **key indicators** shown beside each activity have been developed to give an idea of how long that item might take.

One key indicates a simple introductory activity that is likely to take only a short time to complete.

Two keys indicate a more in-depth activity that will require some thought and time.

Three keys indicate a high-content section containing the main thrust of the teaching.

By choosing more of the one-key activities and fewer of the three-key ones, you will have a shorter session. The reverse, of course, will give a longer session.

A *Core Skills for Family Ministry* session is laid out as follows.

- ✤ **Aim** of the whole module
- ✤ **Learning outcomes** that should be achieved through the session
- ✤ **Materials** needed to run the session
- ✤ **Opening thought** to enable reflection
- ✤ **Starters:** ways into the topic
- ✤ **Core teaching:** the main teaching element
- ✤ **Biblical thought:** tying the teaching to the Bible
- ✤ **Reflection on learning:** a prompt to help better understanding of the session
- ✤ **Worship:** suggestions to close the session in themed worship
- ✤ **Personal reflection sheet** to assist participants in noting their learning outcomes
- ✤ **Portfolio checklist** for those wishing to collect evidence of learning

Keep an eye on the CGMC website www.cgmcontheweb.com for additional resources, web links, articles and book suggestions, which will help participants to expand their knowledge.

Templates and handout sheets can be downloaded at www.barnabasinchurches.org.uk/9780857464316.

Introductory session

Aim

- To provide a basic introduction to working with families in a church context
- To begin to engage participants in the content of the course

Learning outcomes

- To share hopes and fears about working with families
- To reflect critically on a variety of strategies for developing relationships with families
- To explore issues around families, theology and culture
- To consider how to approach a session with families
- To acknowledge and reflect on our personal experiences of family, and to recognise how this might impact on our approach to family ministry

Materials needed

- Labels or name badges for people as they arrive
- Flip chart paper and pens
- Bowl containing a wide variety of fruits, including some more unusual fruits if possible
- Sticky notes
- Pictures of fruit (page 16) or fruit-shaped sticky notes
- Copies of the Assessing training needs questionnaire (page 17)

Opening thought

Hear, O Israel: The Lord our God, the Lord is one. Love the Lord your God with all your heart and with all your soul and with all your strength. These commandments that I give you today are to be on your hearts. Impress them on your children. Talk about them when you sit at home and when you walk along the road, when you lie down and when you get up. Tie them as symbols on your hands and bind them on your foreheads. Write them on the doorframes of your houses and on your gates.
Deuteronomy 6:4–9

Community may be one of the first ways in which we encounter faith in the context of daily life. This may be in a family environment, whether that be biological, extended or church family. Faith can be nurtured and shaped through our experiences of such relationships. In this learning session, the group will develop a better understanding of each other's role in family ministry.

Starters

Who am I?

You will need
- Flip chart paper and pens

Invite those attending to create groups of three and to check that they know each other's names. Then find out about the context of each other's work with families and family ministry.

Invite people to discuss:

- How they each felt before they came to this session.
- Their hopes and concerns about working with families.
- What they hope to get out of this session.

Invite feedback only on the hopes and concerns, which should be written on flip chart paper.

Fruit bowl 

You will need
- Bowl containing a wide variety of fruits, including some more unusual fruits if possible

Place the bowl of fruit at the front or in the centre of the group. Each person states which of the fruits best describes them and why.

This is a reminder that each person brings something different to family ministry, which leads to a balanced and varied combination—as would be the case in a fruit salad.

Ask people:

- How did they feel when they were choosing a piece of fruit?
- What is their role in family ministry? Is it, for example, exciting, daunting or a combination?
- What insight does this gives them in their work with families?

Core teaching

Reflecting on family life

It is important to be sensitive and offer the following as a time for personal reflection as opposed to sharing with the wider group, as it may be a difficult or painful experience for some people.

For many of us, there will have been someone who has influenced us and had an impact on our lives.

Invite people to find their own space and go through the following points:

- What words come to mind when you think about your own experience of family?
- Can you think about a person in your family who was a positive influence, or someone that you learnt from?
- What qualities did that person have that had the most influence on you?
- Think of a family tradition that has stayed with you. For example, for some eating meals in the house anywhere other than the kitchen or dining room would have been unacceptable. For others it may be something different.
- Is this something you still hold to now and has it been passed on to younger generations?
- How do you think your past experience, whether positive or negative, impacts your approach to family ministry?

As part of your portfolio, without going into specific detail, are there things that you have been surprised to remember during these questions and/or are there things you have realised for the first time?

Current context of families 

You will need
- Pictures of fruit (page 16) or fruit-shaped sticky notes

Working in small groups, invite people to write on the fruit shapes the key challenges faced by families they know or work with today, e.g. financial difficulties.

Share findings as a whole group.

Working with families  

Invite people to share the experience of a memorable occasion when they have worked with families. Ask them to consider:

- What worked well, why did it work well and why do they remember it?
- What challenges have they met, or are they anticipating, in their work with families?
- Referring back to the fruit bowl exercise, which three challenges are the most relevant to their work and are they able to address these?

Considerations when working with families

It is important to be aware of a number of factors when working with and supporting families:

✤ Recognise the value of building positive, open and trusting relationships with the families you are working with
✤ Recognise the real difficulties the families face rather than perceived difficulties—taking time to get to know them is an important factor in this
✤ Recognise the importance of starting from where they are and journeying with them

Ask the group to discuss which of these factors is most important to them at this stage in their work.

Which of them presents the greatest challenges?

Assessing training needs  

You will need
❋ Copies of the Assessing training needs questionnaire (page 17)

This session has drawn attention to just some of the skills and knowledge that are important for any adult working with families on behalf of the church. Some of this skill comes with experience, but it is important to take time to do some conscious learning as well, and to reflect critically on your experiences. Look at the outline of these sessions on the questionnaire and fill in the boxes to help you assess which topics are priorities for you.

Biblical thought

Choose a Bible story which does *not* reflect an 'ideal' family situation. Some suggestions are given below.

Joseph's dreams, Genesis 37
Mary and Martha, Luke 10:38–42
The birth of Moses, Exodus 2:1–10
Ruth and Naomi, Ruth 1:1–10
Jesus in the temple, Luke 2:41–52

Ask one/some of the following questions:

✤ What is it that is causing the difficulties?
✤ How does it progress?
✤ Is there a satisfactory resolution?
✤ Are there things we can learn from this for our work with families?

In small groups, invite people to share one aspect of this session that has had a particular impact on them.

Worship

Sing or reflect on the words of the hymn 'Amazing Grace' together. Recognise and give thanks for the grace of God which allows each one of us to be a part of God's family.

Prayer

Heavenly Father
Thank you for the wonder of family—
A place that brings us joy and hope
Laughter and kindness
Yet also sometimes difficulty and frustration
Heartache and worry.

Father, would you dwell
At the heart of all families
As they seek to live life with one another.
Give them love and patience
Guide them in their lives together
Sustain them when life is difficult
Rejoice with them when life is good
And forever be the firm foundation
On which they can trust.

Thank you for your eternal love of us
Thank you for mothers, fathers, brothers, sisters,
Grandparents, cousins, sons, daughters
For all those who care and love
And create family where maybe it
Has been absent.
Give us all a heart to serve, love and cherish our family
As you have loved us.
Amen

Optional activity

Chop up the fruit from the fruit bowl and enjoy together before leaving the session.

Pictures of fruit

Assessing training needs questionnaire

No knowledge: **N** Some knowledge: **S** Fully confident: **F**

Introductory session

- ✤ To share hopes and fears about working with families ☐
- ✤ To reflect critically on a variety of strategies for developing relationships with families ☐
- ✤ To explore issues around families, theology and culture ☐
- ✤ To consider how to approach a session with families ☐
- ✤ To acknowledge and reflect on our personal experiences of family, and to recognise how this might impact on our approach to family ministry ☐

Core Session One: Biblical, historical and contemporary understanding of family

- ✤ To gain insight into the biblical and historical understandings surrounding family ☐
- ✤ To reflect on the differences and similarities between similarities between historical and contemporary situations ☐
- ✤ To reflect on the structure of your own family, and of those around them ☐

Core Session Two: Family ministry today

- ✤ To explore opportunities for families and churches to engage with each other ☐
- ✤ To recognise the contemporary context of family life ☐

Core Session Three: Seasons of family life

- ✤ To recognise the role of the church in the various seasons of family life ☐
- ✤ To reflect on the occasions when families may celebrate and commemorate significant milestones experienced in their lives ☐
- ✤ To appreciate the importance of managing these seasons well ☐
- ✤ To be equipped and gain tools to support and resource families during these seasons of life ☐

Core Session Four: Role of family relationships

- ✤ To reflect on traditional relationships and consider the implications for families if some of these relationships are missing or distorted (for example, mother/child, father/child, husband/wife, grandparent/child, neighbours, siblings, family/school, family/GP, family/vicar) ☐

Assessing training needs questionnaire continued

No knowledge: **N** Some knowledge: **S** Fully confident: **F**

Core Session Four: Role of family relationships continued

- To plan ways to develop and strengthen relationships with families ☐
- To explore how the church might offer specific support to families to help alleviate the impact of a missing or distorted relationship ☐

Core Session Five: Family well-being and wholeness

- To gain a clearer understanding of the influence and impact of well-being on the life of families ☐
- To develop thinking and inform future practice to ensure full participation by families in the life of the church ☐

Core Session Six: Faith in families

- To recognise the role of the church in supporting families to live out faith in the home in a way that is appropriate and accessible for families ☐
- To recognise the different factors to be taken into account when working with families, such as age, experience, time and finance ☐
- To equip leaders to help families create faith-filled homes ☐

CORE SESSION ONE

Biblical, historical and contemporary understanding of family

Aim

- To introduce participants to biblical and contemporary understandings and meanings of family

Learning outcomes

- To gain insight into the biblical and historical understandings surrounding family
- To reflect on the differences and similarities between historical and contemporary situations
- To reflect on the structure of your own family, and of those around them

Materials needed

- A Bible
- Photos of a wide range of family groupings
- Copies of 'Understandings of family' handout sheet (page 23)
- A selection of newspapers (tabloids and broadsheets)
- Copies of body outline template (page 24), pens, scissors to cut out if wished

Opening thought

For the sake of my family and friends, I will say, 'Peace be within you.'
Psalm 122:8

When we use the word 'family', what do we think about or imagine? What exactly is a 'family', and how is it structured?

What we understand about family is important, and often depends on our own culture, background and experience. The first concept to grasp is that family has historically been a flexible concept, and so although we may have a determined view or position on family, it has meant different things at different times.

As Christian readers of scripture we may want to point to a biblical example or ideal, but we will find that difficult as we briefly explore the complexities of Middle Eastern structures reaching back thousands of years. If we explore more recent understandings of family here in Britain we will discover that family structures have changed as society has. Our contemporary understanding is also evolving.

Starter

Icebreaker

You will need
- Photos of a wide range of family groupings

Invite people to choose a photograph from the selection provided and in small groups consider what comes to mind when they look at them.

Give some time for groups to feed back one or two key points from their discussions.

Return to the small groups and ask people to describe their own experience of family in terms of structure. Has this been consistent over the last few generations?

Core teaching

Changing perspectives

You will need
- Copies of 'Understandings of family' handout sheet (page 23)

In this section we are going to spend time looking at families from three viewpoints—biblical, historical and contemporary. Give the handout sheet to participants to follow while sharing the following details.

Biblical understandings of family

We start our exploration by reflecting on *biblical* understandings of family. However, the biblical account covers several thousand years of social development. It moves from Old Testament accounts of early nomadic peoples to the first-century world of the New Testament with its highly structured, class-based societies, influenced not only by their own Jewish religion, but by the cultures of societies around them.

A biblical family life, therefore, in some way depends on which biblical era you are exploring. The context is important, as well as remembering that even over those several thousand years life for nearly all the populations of the Middle East was severely restricted, both geographically and in terms of social mobility. There were several people movements (often due to famine or war), with some individuals travelling across the region, but most people stayed in a very closed area and built up their resources and wealth on lands which were handed down from generation to generation.

Key points

There are some key ideas that emerge in the biblical account surrounding the Israelite people that can help us towards their tribal understanding of family. These are based around understandings of *kinship, clan and tribe*—a broadly Middle Eastern view of family which in many cases still holds today.

- **Multigenerational family structure**
- **Marriage** was a binding agent within the kin and clan
- The role of **family elders**, but especially the elder male in the household was deeply important
- Most families were **producers**, and not just consumers
- Life was built around **large families**, necessary as an investment for future work on the land
- **Infant mortality** was high

Historical understandings of family

Looking to the *historical* development of family from the Victorian era through to 20th-century Britain, there's a very different construct of family, emerging out of ideas around 'the model family' of the Victorian era, often termed the 'nuclear' family. Stronger transport links, wider social movement, greater academic and economic opportunities (especially post 1960s for women), destruction of traditional work patterns, and wider house ownership led to a dispersal of the relational family across the country.

Key points

- **Households** set up outside of the marriage or partners' families
- **Marriage** is by free choice, and in the main is not determined by parents or elders
- **Older generations** are more independent; multigenerational family becomes rarer
- The desire or need for **children** comes into question

Again the context is important, as 20th-century Britain was Western in its philosophy, increasingly post-industrial in its economics, and towards the end of the century much more postmodern, individualistic and consumerist in its choices about a great number of things. This is a significant development for the family, as it raises issues about the desire or need for children or otherwise, and also about the economic purposes and choices which are offered to the next generation.

Contemporary understandings of family

Moving into the 21st century, there has been the growth of developments rooted in the late 20th century, which is having social impact across the generations. A few headlines may help us to think of other developments.

Key points

- **Households:** rise in community groupings
- **Relationships:** increase in divorce, numbers of blended or stepfamilies on the rise
- **Role of adults** in the household is changing, leading to more home-based working, parental role switching, and part-time working
- **Family types:** increasing number of single-parent households. More same-sex partnerships with opportunities to have their own children

Some commentators talk about the fragmentation of the linked family, and living in a disintegrating (anomic) time for the family, while others, emphasising the more flexible and fluid nature of many new households, focus on the evolving diversity and various modes of family structure and point to the importance of relational interconnectedness within the household, however it is constructed.

What does this mean for the church? How does it respond with scriptural integrity, a firm grip on tradition, yet a relevance for today? An interesting question, both in terms of attitudes to those who are existing members of the community and those whom the church is trying to reach.

Family life today 

You will need

- A selection of newspapers (tabloids and broadsheets)

Ask participants to look through the newspapers and discuss what they might tell us about family life today.

Families and change 

You will need

- Body outline (page 24)
- Pens
- Scissors to cut out if wished

Using the outline of a person, ask people to write down the points about families that have made an impact on them and how these points have changed over time.

Biblical thought

You will need

- Copies of 'Understandings of family' handout sheet (page 23)

Jesus himself takes us into some very interesting areas in relation to the family. For anyone raised in the Jewish understandings and traditions of kinship, clan and tribe with its strong emphasis on lineage and genealogy, and with its responsibilities to those within the kinship circle especially, the dialogue in Matthew 12:46–50 (echoed in Luke 8:20–21 and Mark 3:32–35) is an intriguing challenge.

While Jesus was still talking to the crowd, his mother and brothers stood outside, wanting to speak to him. Someone told him, 'Your mother and brothers are standing outside, wanting to speak to you.' He replied to him, 'Who is my mother, and who are my brothers?' Pointing to his disciples, he said, 'Here are my mother and my brothers. For whoever does the will of my Father in heaven is my brother and sister and mother.'

In this dialogue at least, the interconnectedness of those he would call kin relatives is placed in relation to the higher household of his 'Father in heaven'. If 'blood is thicker than water', as we sometimes say, then what type of family is thicker than blood?

Reflection on learning

Invite people to consider:

- Look at the handout sheet. What similarities and differences do you identify across the ages?
- How does your church acknowledge the influence of families down the ages?

Worship

These worship ideas can be used by an individual, or within the group following the time of reflective discussion. Ask participants to reflect on one of the following:

- Who are the people who are important in your life? This may include those not biologically related to you and those who support you. Write their names on the outline of a person.
- As you do this exercise, thank God for the relationships you are describing, and ask God to help and bless any difficulties you have in those relationships.

- ✤ If in a trusted group of friends, maybe a time of describing what you are discovering to someone else would be helpful, as well as hearing about someone else's description of family and praying for them.

Prayer

God, our loving parent,
Help us in our understandings of family.
Be with families close to us, and surrounding us in our communities.
Be with those who see family differently across the world,
and may there be love at the heart of all these relationships.
Help us to recognise our place in your family,
and your place in our households and homes.
Amen

Understandings of family

Biblical *Kinship, clan and tribe*	**Historical** *Development of family in 20th century—the nuclear family*	**Contemporary** *Late 20th to early 21st century*
Multigenerational family structure: relationships with this kinship circle were paramount and above all others.	**Households:** set up outside of the family men and women marry into, creating independent homes. Commentators talk about 'social disintegration' of the family.	**Households:** rise in community groupings of friends and family where several generations live together due to economic and housing costs.
Marriage: binding within the kin and clan. Partners controlled by customs and parents. The dowry (or transfer of wealth) was very important and a matter of family honour and part of a strategy to keep wealth within the wider family.	**Marriage** is a free choice, not determined by parents or elders, and partners are found from different places and social rankings. The word 'marriage' is increasingly replaced by 'partnership'.	**Relationships:** increase in divorce and separation with more households created from two families joining together. Blended or stepfamilies are on the rise.
Family elders, especially the elder male, protected the honour not only of the family name but also the purity of women in the household to ensure that the inheritance was not lost.	**Older generation** become more independent as there is greater care provision available (following rise of social state post-1945). Rare to have multigenerational households.	**Role of adults:** vast change in work patterns and opportunities have led to more home-based working, role switching for parents and part-time working.
Families as producers: life was built around large families. Having children was necessary as an investment for future work on the land.	**Children:** the desire or need for children comes into question as lifestyle choices are more individualistic and economic factors influence the shape of households.	**Family types:** increasing number of single-parent households, some through choice. Same-sex partnerships with opportunities to have their own children are increasingly understood and accepted.
Infant mortality: estimated that less than 50% of children lived to their fifth birthday and only 40% of the population lived to 20 years at the time of Jesus.		

Body outline

CORE SESSION ONE: BIBLICAL, HISTORICAL AND CONTEMPORARY UNDERSTANDING OF FAMILY

Personal reflection sheet

What did you learn from this session?

How will this affect the way you work with families?

What further items in this area would you like to follow up?

CORE SESSION ONE: BIBLICAL, HISTORICAL AND CONTEMPORARY UNDERSTANDING OF FAMILY

Portfolio checklist

Learning outcomes

- ✤ To gain insight into the biblical and historical understandings surrounding family
- ✤ To reflect on the differences and similarities between historical and contemporary situations
- ✤ To reflect on the structure of your own family, and of those around them

Choose two of these learning outcomes. Write down what you have learnt in relation to these and how they might benefit your work with families.

To show that the learning outcomes have been achieved, your portfolio must include at least the following. *(Tick when you have included each one in the file.)*

☐ Personal reflection sheet

☐ Any notes taken during the session, with any additional ideas

☐ Any other responses/reflections you wish to include

The participant's involvement in a group for 'Core Session One: Biblical, historical and contemporary understanding of family' is confirmed.

Signed (assessor)______________________________ Date __________

Any comments from assessor

Signed (candidate)______________________________ Date __________

CORE SESSION TWO

Family ministry today

Aim

- To recognise the importance of relevant work with families in a rapidly changing world

Learning outcomes

- To explore opportunities for families and churches to engage with each other
- To recognise the contemporary context of family life

Materials needed

- 'Traditional' family photo from the 1920s
- Flip charts, paper and pens
- Photos of families from magazines
- Sticky notes
- Two boxes or bags of sweets, one in which every sweet is the same and the other containing a variety, such as a box of Liquorice AllSorts, which includes many different shapes, sizes and flavours
- Copies of 'Bible family descriptions' handout sheet (page 32)
- Copies of body outline template (page 24), pens
- Image of the presentation of Christ in the temple (use an icon or painting, or you could search for images online)
- Strips of coloured paper to make paper chains (A4 cut lengthwise is a good size)
- Pens
- Reflective music

Opening thought

Keep these words that I am commanding you today in your heart. Recite them to your children and talk about them when you are at home and when you are away, when you lie down and when you rise. Bind them as a sign on your hand, fix them as an emblem on your forehead, and write them on the doorposts of your house and on your gates.
Deuteronomy 6:6–9

Starters

Icebreaker 

You will need
- ❋ 'Traditional' family photo from the 1920s

Look at a 'traditional' family photo from the 1920s. What things strike you as you look at it?

What do you know, if anything, about family life back then?

If you have information about what your family was like in the 1920s, think about whether this had a structure similar to the family in the photo.

Compare this with the newly commissioned statue of a modern family that has been erected in Birmingham—www.arealbirminghamfamily.com.

What sorts of families is your church working with?

Changing world

You will need
- ❋ Flip charts, paper and pens
- ❋ Photos of families from magazines
- ❋ Sticky notes

We live in a time unlike any other time that any living person has ever known; it's not merely that things are changing; change itself has changed.

William Easum, *Sacred Cows Make Gourmet Burgers* (Abingdon Press, 1995), p. 21

Do the following in two different groups.

Group one

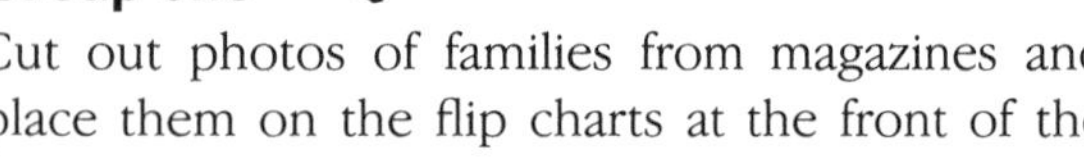

Cut out photos of families from magazines and place them on the flip charts at the front of the room.

Group two

On sticky notes, write down as many types of family as you can think of and place them on the flip charts at the front of the room.

Have a look at the photographs and the sticky notes.

What are the conclusions about family life in 21st-century UK today? Discuss.

Society and its influence 

You will need
- ❋ Flip charts, paper and pens

Think about the changes within society today. What do they look like? Write ideas on flip chart paper.

Discuss the changes together in the wider group.

- ✤ Are there any surprises?
- ✤ What are the implications for family life?
- ✤ How may the changes in society impact ministry to families?

Core teaching

Discussion starters

You will need
- ❋ Two boxes or bags of sweets, one in which every sweet is the same and the other containing a variety, such as a box of Liquorice Allsorts, which includes many different shapes, sizes and flavours

Discussion starter 1 

Families come in all shapes and sizes and increasingly are not one mum and one dad with their one or two biological children.

Talk about the sweets and people's preferences, especially with respect to variety versus sameness.

Link this to the varieties of types of families that we have in the UK today.

Ask your group to identify the many different sorts of family that exist. For example:

- ✤ divided families due to relationship breakdown
- ✤ blended families coming from more than one marriage/partnership
- ✤ single-parent families
- ✤ child-headed households or families in which children are the carers for the adult(s)
- ✤ grandparents looking after grandchildren or stepgrandchildren
- ✤ extended families where more than one 'family' is living together in a shared household
- ✤ cross-cultural families

What others can you think of?

What is the equivalent of the sweets or the liquorice that is common to all these types of families?

Discussion starter 2

Here are some headline statistics on families in the UK today published by the Office of National Statistics (January 2015).

- In 2014 there were 18.6 million families in the UK. Of these, 12.5 million were married couple families. This is the most common family type in the UK.
- Cohabiting couple families grew by 29.7% between 2004 and 2014. This is the fastest growing type of family in the UK.
- In 2014 there were 2.0 million lone parents with dependent children in the UK. Women accounted for 91% of lone parents with dependent children.
- There were 26.7 million households in the UK in 2014. 28% of these contained only one person.
- Households containing two or more families were the fastest growing household type in the decade to 2014, increasing by 56% to 313,000 households.

(For the full statistics go to: www.ons.gov.uk/ons/publications/re-reference-tables.html?edition=tcm%3A77-383612.)

What surprises or interests you in these figures?

Group exercises  

> You will need
> - Copies of 'Bible family descriptions' handout sheet (page 32)

It's important to recognise that the so-called nuclear family is a very modern invention and certainly does not have a particular biblical precedent.

Give the handout sheet, listing six descriptions of a Bible family, to people in your group. Can they work out which Bible story is involved as each is read out?

(Answers: Adam's family, Abraham's family, Isaac's family, Jacob's family, Samuel's family, David's family)

How do these family shapes relate to those they have come across in your ministry?

Consider what sorts of family are defined by the following words:

- A household
- A fellowship
- A network
- A tribe
- A clan
- A commune
- A club
- A cooperative
- A church

Clearly families do not just rely on blood ties but also connections based on culture, friendship and even economic dependence.

Given all this background, how would they describe a family? What sort of social grouping might best nurture children in fullness of life?

Consider this definition of family: *Family is a social network that includes adults and children and which comes together for the nurture of children.*

In this context, consider what sort of families can or could exist in children's homes or orphanages.

Going deeper 

> You will need
> - Copies of body outline template (page 24)
> - Pens

In the context of 'family', it is also interesting to explore what it means to be a parent. In groups of three or four, write on the outline of a person all the positive words linked to the term 'parent' that come to mind.

Compare and discuss the results. How would they describe a parent in one sentence? How does this relate to the word 'family'?

It might help to consider who has 'parented' them in their life and helped nurture them to become the best they can be.

Alternative shapes

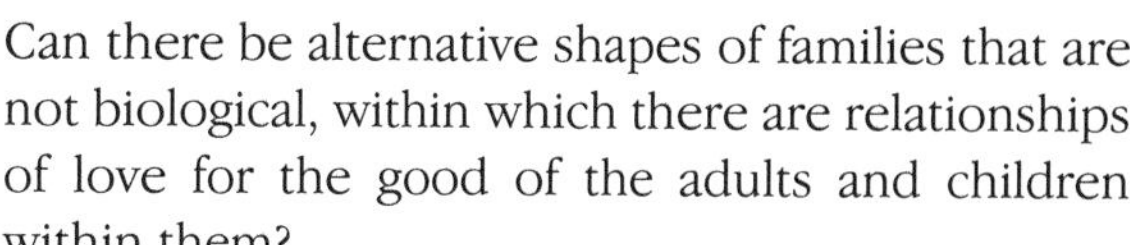

Can there be alternative shapes of families that are not biological, within which there are relationships of love for the good of the adults and children within them?

Can the church at its best be this?

Consider Paul's favoured image of church family as 'the body of Christ'—see Romans 12:3–8 and 1 Corinthians 12:13–31 and Ephesians 4:4–6.

What sort of family is a church congregation?

Five parameters 

Keith White in his book *The Growth of Love* (Barnabas for Children, 2011) sets out five parameters for the nurture of human wholeness.

- Security—a safe place to be
- Significance—being known by name
- Boundaries—having clear limits; protective walls

✤ Creativity—an opportunity to play and explore
✤ Community—a sense of belonging to a bigger group in which you are valued

How can these be realised and developed in some of the family groupings they have been considering?

How can the church be this sort of family, or how can Christians help promote these sorts of values for the families with which they work?

Consider what is undermining family life today. How is the safe nurture of children by adults being jeopardised? What are the threats?

What can Christians either individually or as congregations do to support families in crisis?

From the Bible  

You will need
* Image of the presentation of Christ in the temple (use an icon or painting, or you could search for images online)

Consider two Bible stories about family.

Luke 2:22–39: This story, celebrated in the festival of Candlemas, describes how Jesus is brought as a baby by his mother and earthly father Joseph to the temple where they encounter two older grandparent figures.

Look at an icon or painting of this family and consider the relationships between each of the people present. In what sense is this a family that is beyond ties of blood?

1 Kings 3:16–28: In this story, often cited as an example of Solomon's wisdom, the king is asked to decide on who is the true mother of a baby. The threat to divide the baby in two reveals the real mother as the one with genuine compassion for her child. In an interesting twist to this story, the dramatist Berthold Brecht in his play *The Caucasian Chalk Circle* has a similar scenario but here the true mother to the child turns out not to be its birth mother. See here for a summary of the play: www.gradesaver.com/the-caucasian-chalk-circle/study-guide/summary.

What might this tell us about the true nature of healthy adult/child nurturing within a family relationship?

There are other interesting examples in the Bible of different sorts of families to consider:

✤ The 'family' in the home in Bethany, where two sisters (Mary and Martha) with their brother Lazarus often made Jesus welcome. Note that there are no children present in this context; yet surely this is still a family? Or is it? (See Luke 10:38–42.)
✤ The new relationship inaugurated at the cross when Jesus asks Mary to take John as her new child and John to take Mary as his new mother. (See John 19:25–27.)

Biblical thought

Reflect on family in the Old Testament and the New Testament.

Genesis 4:1–9: 'Am I my brother's keeper?'

Into the family may come the joy of children. They are different personalities; they have different gifts; there is sibling rivalry and jealousy and, in this extreme case, one brother takes the life of the other. God's 'ideal' family fell out with God, and fell out with each other.

✤ How might this speak into the diversity of family life today?

Matthew 1:18–25: '[She] will… give birth to a son, and they will call him Immanuel.'

The beginning of the New Testament, the new story, the new chapter starts once again with God's focus on family. This time he chooses a young girl, engaged to an older man, and comes to earth in order to 'get it right'. This family makes sense because God is in the centre of it. Both parents and extended family are dedicated to God, and into this backdrop, God's Immanuel presence is promised to us and our families.

✤ What one thing might God speak into family life today?

Reflection on learning

✤ What challenges has this session raised in terms of their own understanding of family life in society today?
✤ On reflection, what practical things do they feel the church may be able to consider to encourage engagement with families?

Worship

You will need
- ✻ Strips of coloured paper to make paper chains (A4 cut lengthwise is a good size)
- ✻ Pens
- ✻ Reflective music

Read Psalm 145:1–9.

I will exalt you, my God the King; I will praise your name for ever and ever. Every day I will praise you and extol your name for ever and ever.

Great is the Lord and most worthy of praise; his greatness no one can fathom. One generation commends your works to another; they tell of your mighty acts. They speak of the glorious splendour of your majesty—and I will meditate on your wonderful works. They tell of the power of your awesome works—and I will proclaim your great deeds. They celebrate your abundant goodness and joyfully sing of your righteousness.

The Lord is gracious and compassionate, slow to anger and rich in love.

The Lord is good to all; he has compassion on all he has made.

Sing 'For the beauty of the earth' as a prayer with united prayer at the end of every verse:

'Father, unto thee we raise this our joyful hymn of praise.'

Take a moment to write on the strips of paper the names of people who need prayer. This could be family, friends, church members or wider community members.

Collect these names together and, while reflective music is being played, connect them together into a 'prayer paper chain'. This can act as a positive reminder of today's session over coming weeks.

Benediction

The Lord is gracious and compassionate,
Slow to anger and rich in love.
The Lord is good to all;
He has compassion on all he has made.

Psalm 145:9

Bible family descriptions

A family that included two mums and two stepmums, stepbrothers and stepsisters and also involved sexual abuse and attempted murder

A family blighted by parental favouritism and sibling rivalry

A family that included adultery, murder and later fatal sibling rivalry

A family that included a dad, a mum, a surrogate mum and stepbrothers

A family torn apart by a brother killing a brother

A family that had two mums, a child separated from its mum at an early age and brought up by a second family made up of a grandfather, who also had two delinquent teenage children

CORE SESSION TWO: FAMILY MINISTRY TODAY

Personal reflection sheet

What did you learn from this session?

How will this affect the way you work with families?

What further items in this area would you like to follow up?

CORE SESSION TWO: FAMILY MINISTRY TODAY

Portfolio checklist

Learning outcomes

- To explore opportunities for families and churches to engage with each other
- To recognise the contemporary context of family life

Write down what you have learnt in relation to these learning outcomes and how they might benefit your work with families.

To show that the learning outcomes have been achieved, your portfolio must include at least the following. *(Tick when you have included each one in the file.)*

☐ Personal reflection sheet

☐ Any notes taken during the session, with any additional ideas

☐ Any other responses/reflections you wish to include

The participant's involvement in a group for 'Core Session Two: Family ministry today' is confirmed.

Signed (assessor)________________________ Date __________

Any comments from assessor

Signed (candidate)________________________ Date __________

CORE SESSION THREE

Seasons of family life

Aim

- To reflect on and understand that there are different seasons of life for families, applying this understanding to interaction with families and exploring ways the church can affirm and support them

Learning outcomes

- To recognise the role of the church in the various seasons of family life
- To reflect on the occasions when families may celebrate and commemorate significant milestones experienced in their lives
- To appreciate the importance of managing these seasons well
- To be equipped and gain tools to support and resource families during these seasons of life

Materials needed

- Copies of 'human bingo' grid (page 39), pens
- Copies of 'Questions' handout sheet (page 40), scissors to cut out the different questions
- A cake (optional)
- Laptop and projector for showing film clips
- Copies of 'Family development' handout sheet (page 41)
- Copies of the 'Stages of a tree' handout sheet (page 42)
- Copies of 'Significant moments' pictures handout sheet (see page 43)
- Party items, for example, balloons, paper plates, blowers, hats
- Prayer card (page 44)

Opening thought

Rejoice with those who rejoice; mourn with those who mourn.
Romans 12:15

All families experience different seasons of life, and the way they interact during those different seasons together is important for their well-being as a family as well as individually. The church has a vital role in encouraging and supporting parents, carers and children as they encounter these times.

Starters

Icebreaker 

You will need
* Copies of 'human bingo' grid (page 39)
* Pens
* Copies of 'Questions' handout sheet (page 40)
* Scissors to cut out the different questions
* A cake (optional)

Give each person a copy of the 'human bingo' grid and ask them to find someone in the room who corresponds to one of the items on the grid. Tick it off and continue until all nine boxes are complete. A prize could be offered, such as a cake to be shared in the next activity.

Invite people to collect a question and, when everyone has one, to ask one another that question, then swap in order to ask someone else.

Core teaching

Family development

You will need
* Laptop and projector for showing film clips

Choose one (or all) of the following film clips to show, from DVDs or from YouTube:

* *The Incredibles* (Disney Pixar)—family mealtime scene
* *Father of the Bride* (Buena Vista)—the wedding scene
* *Up* (Disney Pixar)—Carl and Ellie married life scene

Families are all different, as we reflected in previous sessions; our lives together as households can vary hugely. Family life is never static. We may be able to anticipate particular periods or seasons, for instance when a child is born or starts school. Many of these contain occasions that are a cause for thanks and celebration but there are often unexpected events that occur which may shake the foundations of our lives together, such as illness and bereavement. We are now going to explore what these various seasons of life are and ways we can meaningfully engage with families at these times.

Different stages 

You will need
* Copies of 'Family development' handout sheet (page 41)

Invite people to work in small groups or pairs, look at the different stages and consider:

* Do you recognise them?
* In your experience, which most closely resembles a family you know and work with?

Each stage has what can be called 'expected norms' and when these change, it often indicates that a new phase is being entered. For many families these transitions can be stressful times. Families do better when they know what to expect of a new stage.

Supporting through transitions 

Invite people to work in small groups, choose one of the stages and consider:

* What difficulties may occur as a family transitions into the next stage?
* How might you intentionally support a family and prepare them for this transition?
* What strategies could you develop?

Viewing family development in this way has its limitations as it takes the model of the traditional or nuclear family as the starting point. Previous assumptions about families being married couples with children no longer reflect the norm in British society today—family structures have changed. Currently more than a third of children do not live in this family structure. As a result, the stages of family development don't automatically follow or progress in such a straightforward manner and cannot necessarily be applied to all families.

Life for families changes over time. All families experience different phases as they develop together, and these will vary depending on their situations and who the members of the household are. Each person will respond differently and families may value support as they encounter challenges during these seasons of life together. It's important to remember that not all families will experience the same seasons in the same way.

Churches can have a key role in supporting families as they experience different stages—both as they join with families to celebrate milestones and as they demonstrate empathy and encouragement during stressful or difficult circumstances. This can have a big impact on family well-being, help develop strong relationships between family members and promote an environment for all to thrive in.

The church's role

Invite people to work in small groups, choose one of the stages and discuss the following statement. Do you agree or disagree with this?

Churches need to take an active role in creating and nurturing family relationships that include but go beyond the marital and parenting roles of the nuclear family. Thus we need a model of family development that fits all families, not just the nuclear family during the first half of life.

Diana Garland, *Family Ministry: A comprehensive guide* (IVP, 2012), p. 123

Seasons of family life tree 

> You will need
> * Copies of the 'Stages of a tree' handout sheet (page 42)

Invite people to use this as a personal reflection activity.

Using the diagram of a tree in different seasons, choose one of the stages of family development.

- Which 'season' do you feel inclined to put the stage in?
- Jot down the kinds of events or milestones that may occur during this season of family life.

Thinking of a family you know or work with, reflect on the experience from a child/young person's or adult's perspective.

- How would it be different for each of them?
- What insights has this given you about the different seasons of family life?
- Where might specific challenges occur?

Significant moments

Within different seasons there will be specific occasions and significant moments. The following activities are designed to help you explore these in more depth.

Reflections on seasons 

> You will need
> * Copies of 'Significant moments' pictures handout sheet (see page 43)

Invite people to work in pairs.

- Choose a picture and discuss what this brings to mind. Explore how these moments may be understood differently by each of us.
- Reflect on how these may be positive for some and difficult for others.
- How may we have encountered this in our roles and ministry?
- What can we do as church to build family identity/cohesion during these seasons?

The church as family 

Invite people to work in pairs.

Choose one of the significant moments in a family's life (use the pictures if this is helpful).

- How can whole church be 'family' during these times?
- Consider ways to support, care or celebrate depending on the occasion that's been chosen.
- What would you need to be aware of, bearing in mind the diversity of family types that exist today?
- Devise a number of steps and ways that the church could respond to a family's needs at this moment.

Joys and challenges 

Invite people to work in small groups.

- Look at one of the stages of development or seasons of life, and identify when there may be significant moments during that time, for example, during the toddler years: a parent returns to work, a sibling arrives, first day at nursery, moving home or area.
- What might be the joys or challenges of one of these moments?
- In what ways could the church enrich the joyful times?
- What support or help may a family appreciate during the challenging times?

The response will clearly depend on the members of the household and their circumstances, so what is valued or needed by one family may not necessarily be the same for another. It's important to consider the nature of the family before responding.

Family traditions 

Families often create their own traditions and celebrate special occasions together such as birthdays or family nights. It's important to value these and encourage families to develop their own ways to do this as it nurtures a sense of family belonging. This also reflects our understanding of what it means to belong to the family of God.

Family rituals foster security and highlight the things that make each family special. They help us to be open to a good God who also gives us security and sees us as special.

Share with one another something from your own experience: a family tradition or time when you celebrated a special occasion. Reflect on how you felt about this.

Use the above and/or the exercise below.

Sacred spaces and rituals of the everyday

A class of children was set a task to create a sacred space in their home. One young girl went home, collected pebbles and leaves, found a cross and a Bible and set these out on the lid of the toilet in their downstairs cloakroom. When asked why she had chosen that place she said, 'Everyone goes in there. They have peace and quiet and time to be with God. And everyone who comes to the house will know we make time for God.'

- ✤ How might you have reacted if you'd been her parent?
- ✤ How might a sacred space be created in your home?
- ✤ How might you encourage other families to make 'peace and quiet and time to be with God'?

Being thankful 

Being thankful—when and how might a family find ways to do this which are a natural part of their daily lives? What could be the barriers to doing this for those families? Imagine a way to encourage families to be thankful. Think of an idea or resource that they could use.

Biblical thought

Read Ruth 1:1–18.

What can be learnt from this passage about the impact and challenges of changes in family life? What might it say about the importance of marking transitions from different seasons of life and the place of wider community in helping to mark this?

Reflection on learning

Some of what has been shared may have been difficult or reminded people of tough circumstances from their own experiences of being family. Take a few moments now to bring these thoughts and feelings to God.

- ✤ How have the discussions in this session impacted your own thinking on the importance of seasons in family life?
- ✤ When might it be appropriate for you and/or the church to be involved?
- ✤ How well do you think your church currently supports families in various seasons of life?
- ✤ How might support be offered at other times?

Worship

You will need
- ✻ Party items, for example, balloons, paper plates, blowers, hats
- ✻ Prayer card (page 44)

Create a celebratory atmosphere by using balloons and party hats, laying the table for a party, and so on. Invite participants to join the party. Place the images used in the 'significant moments' section at the centre of the gathering or ask people to choose one if numbers allow.

Return to the opening thought and read Romans 12:15. How does this contribute or shape our understanding of transitions in family life?

Have a moment of quiet and then use this reflection based on Ecclesiastes 3. It can be distributed as a prayer card for participants to keep (see page 44).

This may be read by one person or go round the group. There may be a pause between each section for people to pray for themselves or for any families that particularly come to mind. If wished, the first and final sentences could be said together.

In every family there are seasons
and moments of significance.
Times to celebrate life
and times to mourn loss.
Seasons of laughter
and seasons of sadness.
Times of new beginnings
and times of final endings.
Moments of unexpected joy
and moments of unwanted trauma.
Times to draw close together
and times of letting go.
Seasons of harmony
and seasons of discord.
Moments to look forward with hope
and moments to look back with thanksgiving.
Lord of the seasons,
God in the moment,
we bring you our worship and praise.

'Human bingo' grid

B I N G O

Been to a school sports day	Family members in another country	Knows someone doing GCSEs
Changed a nappy	Received a card made by a child	Visited an older relative recently
Helped a family member move house	Been to a relative's wedding	Knows a teenager learning to drive

Questions

What do you remember from your first day at school?

What's your favourite day of the week and why?

Where were you living at age eleven?

Share a memorable day out.

When you were growing up, what was your favourite meal?

If you were a cake, what would you be?

What's the best party you've ever been to?

As a teenager, what clothes did you most like to wear?

Share a funny story or embarrassing moment involving your family.

Name your favourite TV family.

Family development

Research has been carried out to understand better how families develop and how their lives change over time. A variety of theories exist that seek to define family life and the stages families experience. This moves beyond the experiences of individuals, recognising that families exist as groups, with members interacting with each other.

Duvall & Hill[1] and Carter & McGoldrick[2] suggested linear stages of development that families pass through.

- Stage 1: beginning families, couple with no children
- Stage 2: childbearing families
- Stage 3: families with preschool children
- Stage 4: families with school-age children
- Stage 5: families with adolescents
- Stage 6: families as launching centres
- Stage 7: families in the middle years
- Stage 8: ageing families

Duvall & Hill

- Leaving home (single young adults)
- Joining of families in marriage
- Families with young children
- Families with adolescents
- Launching children and moving on
- Families in later life

Carter & McGoldrick

Joan Aldous[3] described a 'family career' or family life cycle that implies the same or similar stages are experienced at different times. Alongside the linear models of family development there are also frameworks that take the form of a spiral, involving different generations at different points in a family's life. These frameworks continue to be debated and research is ongoing as to how family life changes and progresses.

As Diana Garland[4] has indicated:

Stage theory is helpful in showing that families in the same stage or stage transitions experience similar challenges and can be expected to respond to those challenges in some predictable ways. Stage theory also points out that the roles and norms of family life do not remain static but change over time. The role of mother and father is continuous, but it also changes in content from birth through childhood and adolescence and on through the stages of adulthood and ageing.

1 Evelyn Duvall & Reuben Hill, 'Report of the Committee on the Dynamics of Family Interaction' (paper presented at the National Conference on Family Life, Washington, 1948)

2 Betty Carter & Monica McGoldrick, *The Changing Family Life Cycle* (Allyn & Bacon, 1989), pp. 3–28

3 Joan Aldous, *Family Careers: Rethinking the developmental perspective* (SAGE Publications, 1996)

4 Diana Garland, *Family Ministry: A comprehensive guide* (IVP, 2012), p. 187

Stages of a tree

Significant moments

Reproduced with permission from *Core Skills for Family Ministry* by CGMC (Barnabas for Children, 2015) www.barnabasinchurches.org.uk

Prayer card

In every family there are seasons
and moments of significance.
Times to celebrate life
and times to mourn loss.
Seasons of laughter
and seasons of sadness.
Times of new beginnings
and times of final endings.
Moments of unexpected joy
and moments of unwanted trauma.
Times to draw close together
and times of letting go.
Seasons of harmony
and seasons of discord.
Moments to look forward with hope
and moments to look back with thanksgiving.
Lord of the seasons,
God in the moment
we bring you our worship and praise.

Prayer card

In every family there are seasons
and moments of significance.
Times to celebrate life
and times to mourn loss.
Seasons of laughter
and seasons of sadness.
Times of new beginnings
and times of final endings.
Moments of unexpected joy
and moments of unwanted trauma.
Times to draw close together
and times of letting go.
Seasons of harmony
and seasons of discord.
Moments to look forward with hope
and moments to look back with thanksgiving.
Lord of the seasons,
God in the moment
we bring you our worship and praise.

Personal reflection sheet

What did you learn from this session?

How will this affect the way you work with families?

What further items in this area would you like to follow up?

CORE SESSION THREE: SEASONS OF FAMILY LIFE

Portfolio checklist

Learning outcomes

- ✤ To recognise the role of the church in the various seasons of family life
- ✤ To reflect on the occasions when families may celebrate and commemorate significant milestones experienced in their lives
- ✤ To appreciate the importance of managing these seasons well
- ✤ To be equipped and gain tools to support and resource families during these seasons of life

Choose two of these learning outcomes. Write down what you have learnt in relation to these and how they might benefit your work with families.

To show that the learning outcomes have been achieved, your portfolio must include at least the following. *(Tick when you have included each one in the file.)*

☐ Personal reflection sheet

☐ Any notes taken during the session, with any additional ideas

☐ Any other responses/reflections you wish to include

The participant's involvement in a group for 'Core Session Three: Seasons of family life' is confirmed.

Signed (assessor)______________________________ Date __________

Any comments from assessor

Signed (candidate)______________________________ Date __________

CORE SESSION FOUR

Role of family relationships

Aim

- To understand the role of relationships within families and between families and their community, including the church
- To explore how the church might offer additional support where relationships are missing or dysfunctional

Learning outcomes

- To reflect on traditional relationships and consider the implications for families if some of these relationships are missing or distorted (for example, mother/child, father/child, husband/wife, grandparent/child, neighbours, siblings, family/school, family/GP, family/vicar)
- To plan ways to develop and strengthen relationships with families
- To explore how the church might offer specific support to families to help alleviate the impact of a missing or distorted relationship

Materials needed

- Bags of jelly babies
- Paper plates (one for for each group)
- Copies of 'People outlines' template (page 50)
- Scissors
- Flip chart paper and pens
- 'Abraham Maslow's Hierarchy of Needs' handout sheet (page 51)
- A4 paper
- Felt pens or biros

Opening thought

Sing to God, sing in praise to his name... A father to the fatherless, a defender of widows... God sets the lonely in families.
Psalm 68:4–6

Starters

Me and my family 

You will need
- ✻ Bags of jelly babies
- ✻ Paper plates (one for each group)

Invite people to work in groups.

Ask them to take it in turns to use the jelly babies and the plate to explain to everyone about the different people who are present in their family (this could be their family when growing up, or their family as it looks now). After everyone has had a turn, ask them to think about the following questions:

- ✤ What are the similarities between your families?
- ✤ What are the differences between your families?
- ✤ How are the different people in the families related (for example, are they all blood relatives)?

Paper people 

You will need
- ✻ Copies of 'People outlines' template (page 50)
- ✻ Scissors

Families come in all sorts of different shapes and sizes. Use the people outlines provided to make up lots of different examples of family groups.

- ✤ Who are the different people that are represented in the family groups you have created?
- ✤ What are the roles of the people in those groups?

Core teaching

God's plan for families 

You will need
- ✻ Flip chart paper and pens
- ✻ 'Abraham Maslow's Hierarchy of Needs' handout sheet (page 51)

The importance of family in God's plan is evident right from the beginning of the Bible. In Genesis 1:26–28, God creates humans and commissions them to go forth and multiply. This decision by God automatically ensures that all new life is welcomed into the world in the context of a family, with older generations taking responsibility for nurturing babies and children and, as a result, intergenerational communities are formed. Ask people to use a large sheet of flip chart paper to make a list of all of the functions of family relationships that they can think of.

Once the list is completed, rank the functions in order of importance.

Compare the list to that of Abraham Maslow's Hierarchy of Needs.

What elements of Maslow's theory do you agree with? What elements (if any) would you like to challenge?

It takes a whole church to raise a child 

You will need
- ✻ Paper people families from previous activity

There is an African proverb that states, 'It takes a whole village to raise a child.' Sometimes we can become ingrained in thinking about family just as a unit that includes two generations, most usually parents and children; however, this is a very 21st-century Western view of family. Mark Griffiths, in his book *One Generation from Extinction* (Monarch Books, 2009), provides a helpful overview of different translations of the word 'family' in the Bible.

Griffiths states that occasionally the Hebrew word *bah'-ith* is used to describe family relationships; this refers to the concept of parents and children, the view of the immediate family that we are most likely to describe when asked what family looks like. *Bah'-ith* is used in Exodus 12:21–28 where the instructions for the Passover meal are given. However, the most common Hebrew word translated as family that is used within the Bible is *mish-paw-khaw*. This word carries with it a sense of tribe or clan, a multi-generational community that is united by a bond of kinship rather than just blood relatives. Deuteronomy 6:5–7 and 11:18–19 include *mish-paw-khaw* and therefore encourage an intergenerational community approach to passing the faith on to the next generation.

Therefore, family in the Bible has more in common with church than it does with the nuclear family.

Using the paper people families that you created in the starter activity, label each of them as either *bah'-ith* or *mish-paw-khaw*.

Share with the rest of the group how you labelled your families and why.

- ✤ Thinking about your own church, what are the activities you do to encourage *bah'-ith* relationships?

- ✤ What are the activities you do to encourage *mish-paw-khaw* relationships?
- ✤ Are there new ministry possibilities that come to mind when you think about the opportunities to encourage *mish-paw-khaw* relationships?

Relationships that last 

You will need
- ❋ A4 paper
- ❋ Felt pens or biros

In their book *Sticky Faith* (Zondervan, 2011), Dr Kara E. Powell and Dr Chap Clark explain the research conducted by the Fuller Youth Institute to help identify best practices that can help children and young people develop a faith that lasts a lifetime. One of the six recommendations is to build a web of relationships between children, young people and adults; this is *mish-paw-khaw* in action! Very often when working with children and young people, we think about ratios of adults to children (for example, for every five children in the room we need one adult). This challenges us to turn this around... what if for every one child there were five adults caring for each child or young person?

Invite people to work in pairs.

Ask them to draw around their own hand, and write down the names of the people who have most influenced them in their lives.

Invite the pairs to talk about who these people were/are and what they did to influence their faith.

Families should be a place of caring for each other and sharing with each other. However, the reality is that this is not the case in many family situations. There are many children and young people who do not have a family where they can be supported and feel safe.

Ask them to draw around their partner's right hand and think of five children or young people whose lives and faith journey they could invest in. These may well be children with whom they already have a relationship, because they know their parents/carers.

Biblical thought

Read Deuteronomy 6:4–9. Knowing that this passage was written to the entire nation of Israel instead of to individual sets of parents changes the way these commands are viewed. Being a Christian means being part of a *mish-paw-khaw* community, giving responsibility not only to care for each other but also to pass faith on to the next generation. Consider the following questions:

- ✤ How does this passage challenge the way that we do church?
- ✤ How can church become an intergenerational community in which members can support one another, embracing each other as family and committing to walking through life together?

In the light of Deuteronomy 6, read Luke 2:41–52. Knowing that Jesus was part of a *mish-paw-khaw* community is helpful to understand why Mary and Joseph didn't realise they had lost him. It wasn't unusual for Jesus not to be with his parents because he had spiritual aunts and uncles, grandparents and cousins who were involved in his everyday life.

Ask people to consider how their church can help to encourage these types of relationships.

Reflection on learning

Ask participants:
- ✤ If you had to arrange your jelly baby family again, would it look any different in the light of what has been explored in this session?
- ✤ What are the family relationships that God is asking you to stand in the gap for? How might you go about implementing these relationships?

Worship

You will need
- ❋ Handprints from the 'Relationships that last' session
- ❋ Paper people families from starter activity

Invite people to put their handprints in the centre.

Read Psalm 68:4–6 together. Recognise that there is so much to be thankful to God for.

Invite people to think about what it would mean to be *mish-paw-khaw* community.

Invite each person to pick up a handprint belonging to someone else.

Hold that print in the palm of their hand.

Pray for the person or people on the paper. Pray for those children, young people, and adults in their community who are lonely, father- or mother-less or widowed, and ask God to inspire their church in ways of responding to those needs.

Take all of the paper families and place them on a table all together in one big group. This is a visual representation of the church community. Pray over these people that God would help everyone to become a *mish-paw-khaw* community, standing in the gaps where there are missing relationships.

People outlines

Abraham Maslow's Hierarchy of Needs

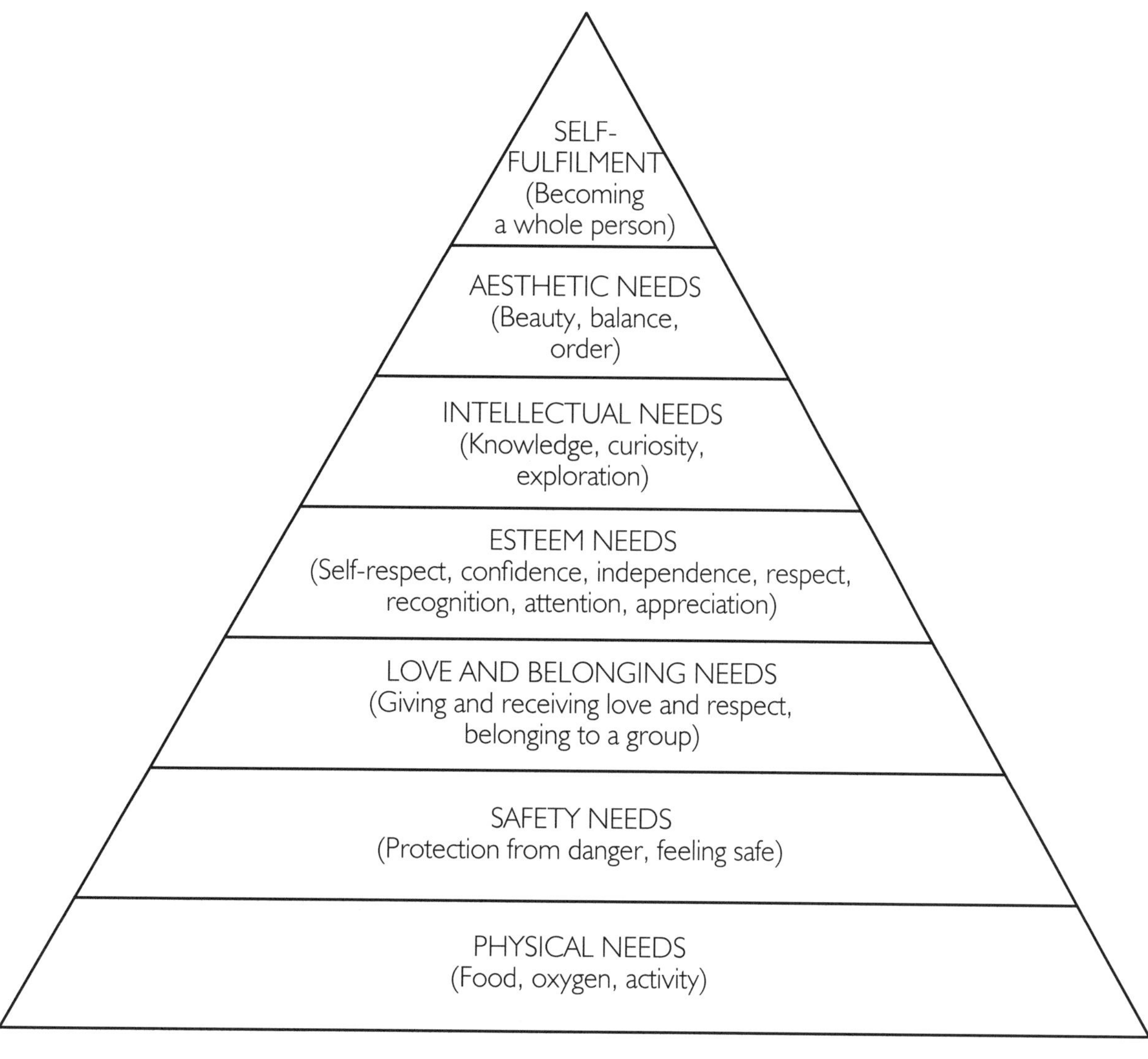

CORE SESSION FOUR: ROLE OF FAMILY RELATIONSHIPS

Personal reflection sheet

What did you learn from this session?

How will this affect the way you work with families?

What further items in this area would you like to follow up?

CORE SESSION FOUR: ROLE OF FAMILY RELATIONSHIPS

Portfolio checklist

Learning outcomes

- To reflect on traditional relationships and consider the implications for families if some of these relationships are missing or distorted (for example, mother/child, father/child, husband/wife, grandparent/child, neighbours, siblings, family/school, family/GP, family/vicar)
- To plan ways to develop and strengthen relationships with families
- To explore how the church might offer specific support to families to help alleviate the impact of a missing or distorted relationship

Choose two of these learning outcomes. Write down what you have learnt in relation to these and how they might benefit your work with families.

To show that the learning outcomes have been achieved, your portfolio must include at least the following. *(Tick when you have included each one in the file.)*

☐ Personal reflection sheet

☐ Any notes taken during the session, with any additional ideas

☐ Any other responses/reflections you wish to include

The participant's involvement in a group for 'Core Session Four: Role of family relationships' is confirmed.

Signed (assessor)______________________________ Date __________

Any comments from assessor

Signed (candidate)______________________________ Date __________

CORE SESSION FIVE

Family well-being and wholeness

Aim

- To understand what subjective well-being is for children and young people
- To understand which aspects of life have the greatest influence on children and young people's well-being
- To consider how the church can listen to and involve families, children and young people to improve and support the collective well-being of families

Learning outcomes

- To gain a clearer understanding of the influence and impact of well-being on the life of families
- To develop thinking and inform future practice to ensure full participation by families in the life of the church

Materials needed

- Flip chart and pens
- Bowl of sweets or chocolates
- Copies of 'Relationships' handout sheet (page 59)
- Sets of prioritisation cards (page 60)
- Copies of 'Family well-being' handout sheet (page 61)
- Copies of 'Choice' handout sheet (page 63)

Opening thought

Well-being is about so much more than happiness, going right to the very heart of a good quality of life. And a real understanding of well-being must also take into account the factors associated with it; the potential drivers. Children with low well-being are not grumpy teenagers experiencing the everyday ups and downs of growing up. Our research highlights stubborn and persistent issues of bullying, insecurity and anxiety; children growing up with little hope for their future.

Matthew Reed, Chief Executive of The Children's Society, *The Good Childhood Report* 2014, p. 5

Starters

Pick and mix 

You will need
* Bowl of sweets or chocolates

Go around the group with the bowl and invite some people to select a sweet.

Randomly select individuals to whom you give a sweet, and others whom you simply look at and walk past.

Afterwards, invite people to reflect on how it felt to have a choice, how it felt to have no choice and how it felt to receive nothing at all.

Talk about the reality of life for some children.

Where do you stand? 

This is a simple activity to encourage people to listen to each other and share opinions.

Begin by saying that there are no right or wrong answers and set a clear time limit for the activity.

Ask everyone in the group to stand up and form a line facing you.

Explain that one wall or end of the line represents 'agree' and the other 'disagree'.

The facilitator makes a statement

Each participant is to show 'where they stand' in relation to the statement by choosing to be closer to the agree or disagree side of the room.

Participants can stand anywhere along the line. For example, if they are undecided, they can stand in the middle.

Ask a few people why they have chosen to stand where they have.

Statements might include:

✤ Pizza is better than chips
✤ Football is more skilled than rugby
✤ It is better to leave school with five good friends than with five good GCSEs
✤ Children these days are much more materialistic compared to children 30 years ago
✤ Families that eat together, stay together

Core teaching

Priorities

You will need
* Copies of 'Relationships' handout sheet (page 59)
* Sets of prioritisation cards (page 60). Print out enough to enable the group to share between five or six participants

Extensive research by The Children's Society shows that relationships are what matters most to children and young people. In The Good Childhood® Inquiry published in 2009, 'family', 'friends', 'love' and 'relationships' were the most frequently used words throughout the 35,000 contributing pieces of evidence. Though many children are affected by changing family structures, the quality of the relationships within their family is more significant to their experiences of childhood than the family structure itself.

Divide into small groups with around five or six people.

Give each group a set of prioritisation cards. These feature seven important aspects of childhood: Education, Love, Family, Money, Material Goods, Safety and Friendship.

Ask each group to consider what they think all children need for a good childhood and to place the cards in order of priority. Give them approximately 10–15 minutes to choose their order.

Invite the groups to share their hierarchy.

Then ask them to repeat the exercise, this time imagining they are a group of children considering their own priorities. How might their ranking order change?

End by explaining that children and adults both tend to prioritise the relationships in their lives. This is something The Children's Society has learnt through The Good Childhood® Inquiry and their well-being research programme.

Go through the 'Relationships' handout sheet and invite people to discuss or comment on the findings.

Relationships 

You will need
* Copies of family well-being handout sheet (page 61)

The Children's Society worked in partnership with the New Economics Foundation to develop five ways to well-being for children and young people: **connect, be active, be creative and play, learn** and **take notice**.

Use the 'Family well-being' handout sheet to consider:

✤ How might your church facilitate this kind of relationship-building for families?

Read John's story.

John and his mum had experienced many tough times together and as a result they had become inseparable. Although this bond was a real strength, it also had its downsides. John struggled to make friends and was getting in trouble at school because of his behaviour. So they approached our mentoring project, where John told us that he'd 'like people to see me for me, and not for the trouble I get into'. His mentor told us: 'John dislikes dogs, so to help him overcome this fear we took my dog to the beach. It was great! John didn't stop laughing and smiling and he loved every minute of it.' He also started attending the project's Friday Club, where he made new friends and used his creative talents to produce some fantastic pieces of artwork. John has made amazing improvements in school and his friendship networks are now much wider.

The work has also helped his relationship with his mum. She is now working, studying and can use some of her spare time to plan and enjoy activities with her daughter, which she couldn't before. She feels that 'things are going their way for once'.

Think about the children and families you know.

- How do their relationships affect their engagement with others?
- How might you encourage an openness really to see and hear the needs of the children in your church?

Money, money, money 

Linking back to the prioritisation activity earlier, adults often assume that children and young people prioritise material goods. Research and consultations by The Children's Society do not show this. In early consultations with children in 2005 it became clear that while money and possessions were viewed as an important ingredient of a good childhood, children emphasised the importance of 'having enough' rather than being rich (*The Good Childhood Report* 2012, p. 25).

Having a similar amount of money to one's friends is linked to higher well-being, and children who have a lot more or less money than their peers feel less happy with their lives as a whole. It's often about a sense of belonging, feeling as though you fit in with your peers, which links back to the significance of relationships and friendships (p. 29).

Consider:

- How might the pressure to have what others have impact on family life?
- What pressure does this put on parents or carers?
- How might the church family help ease or escalate the impact of peer comparisons?

My choice   

You will need

- Copies of 'Choice' handout sheet (page 63)

In addition to the amount of harmony and support within families, parental control also has a significant impact on children's well-being (*The Good Childhood Report* 2013, p. 24).

Invite small groups to discuss the following:

- How does your church listen to children and young people and families?
- How might you support families in giving children real and relevant choices?
- How might your church support the freedom of children and young people to make choices on behalf of themselves and that may impact on others?
- How much does the church feed back changes which come about as a result of listening?

Biblical thought

In Luke 2:41–52 Jesus' parents lost their child on a journey. Imagine their worry! Imagine what others might have said about them—some gossiping about them being bad parents, others sharing their concern. Meanwhile Jesus is in the temple, apparently oblivious to the worry and fear his absence has caused. Yet, it was clear that he needed to be in the temple.

Fear, distraction, worry, reputation, frustration are all words relevant both to the passage and to parenting today. According to The Children's Society research, the three aspects of life which have the greatest influence on well-being today are money and material possessions, choice and autonomy, and relationships. So, for parents, there is a constant juggling between keeping their children 'safe' and allowing them freedom of choice and independence of action.

Invite people to reflect on their own and then share their ideas with one other person.

- What comfort does the Bible reading offer to parents?
- What challenges do parents face in contemporary society?
- How might church communities support young people in achieving positive well-being in the three identified areas?

Reflection on learning

As well as considering how you as a church can support families and promote positive changes within the church, it is important to remember that children are active members of families and the wider society. They identify issues and concerns that adults may not notice or value and should also be engaged meaningfully in any changes in their church or home environment. Armed with this information, we can work together to support families both within and beyond our church communities.

Worship

Read the story of Jesus getting lost in the temple, Luke 2:41–52.

Invite half of the group to take a moment alone to think of negative comments that might have been made to Mary and Joseph, perhaps by fellow travellers, or those in the temple listening to Jesus.

Invite the other half of the group to take a moment alone to think of supportive and encouraging comments that might have been made to Mary and Joseph. The comments should be only a few words, for example, 'leave him alone,' 'his Father's work'.

Ask the 'negative' people to stand in a line beside each other.

Ask the 'positive' people to stand in a line beside each other facing the negative group.

Invite a volunteer to take on the role of Mary or Joseph.

They should walk slowly down the aisle between the groups. Meanwhile everyone simply whispers their chosen phrase over and over. The person walking down the aisle should hear the comments from both sides.

Allow as many people as would like to walk the aisle. Provide opportunity for them to share their experience.

End with a prayer.

Loving God, who parents us all with your desire for our well-being,
Empower those who are parents in our communities to ignore the cacophony of noise and judgement as they follow your lead in encouraging their children to do your work.
Help us to create places where children and young people are welcomed and safe, where they can form strong relationships of trust and understanding and be encouraged to make good, independent choices based on a security of support and love. Amen

Relationships

The Children's Society research programme has highlighted the importance of the quality of family relationships to children's subjective well-being. The quality of the relationships within a family has more of an influence on children's and young people's well-being than the structure of the family. The quality of family relationships explains ten times more of the variation in overall well-being of children than family structure.[1]

Consultations with children and young people in 2005 to 2008 identified good quality relationships with family, friends and others as being of paramount importance in children's own views of what constitutes a good childhood.[2]

Children with low well-being are over 20 times less likely than other children to feel safe at home and eight times more likely to say that their family does not get along well together.[3]

Children need time, not stuff. Linking back to the prioritisation task, we often assume that children prioritise 'things' above 'relationships'. UNICEF research, comparing Britain, Spain and Sweden, paints a picture of a country which has its priorities wrong. A BBC news article summarises UNICEF research from 2011, based on the report card of the previous year, where the UK was bottom of the league for children's well-being out of the 21 most developed countries in the world.[4]

Specific parenting behaviours may impact on the well-being of children aged 14 to 15 years old. The behaviours are divided into four main areas: supervision, physical care, emotional support and educational support. Initial findings indicated that the areas covered under emotional support, such as praise for doing well or support when upset, had the strongest link to children's well-being. The areas covered under supervision, such as making sure you went to school or asking where you were going when you went out, had the weakest association with young people's subjective well-being.[5]

The amount of choice and autonomy afforded to children and young people within the family also has an impact on their well-being. This is discussed further in the choice and autonomy section (see page 63).

The Good Childhood® Inquiry found that a good friend is like 'finding treasure' and, sadly, that fewer children are able to report having one good friend. Through local research and consultations we have learnt that children, particularly young people, want opportunities to nurture their friendships. They rarely request structured, supervised youth provision, such as youth clubs or sports facilities, rather a need for opportunities and venues to 'hang out' and legitimately be. There has been a sharp fall in girls' satisfaction with their friends since 2008.[6]

[1] The Good Childhood Report 2012, p. 18, www.childrenssociety.org.uk/sites/default/files/tcs/good_childhood_report_2012_final_0.pdf

[2] The Good Childhood Report 2013, p. 24

[3] The Good Childhood Report 2013: A summary of our findings, p. 3, www.childrenssociety.org.uk/sites/default/files/tcs/good_childhood_report_-_summary_2013_final.pdf

[4] www.bbc.co.uk/news/uk-14899148

[5] The Good Childhood Report 2014: The executive summary, p. 9, www.childrenssociety.org.uk/sites/default/files/publications/the_good_childhood_report_2014_summary_final.pdf

[6] *A Good Childhood* by Richard Layard and Judy Dunn (Penguin, 2009), pp. 24–25, www.childrenssociety.org.uk/what-we-do/research/initiatives/good-childhood-inquiry/buy-book)

Prioritisation cards

Money	Love	Friendship	Material Goods
Safety	Family	Education	

Family well-being

CONNECT

What we know

7 per cent of children who talk to their family about things that matter to them on most days or every day have low well-being. But for those who never or hardly ever do so, this rises to 28 per cent.

What you can do

One of the hardest things to do as a parent is to slow down and find the time to talk with and listen to our children, no matter what their age.

Unfortunately, the solutions haven't really changed. Shared mealtimes, fewer hours in front of kids' TV and finding activities that the family can enjoy together will all help to support your child's well-being. The same is true of making the time to spend with extended family.

But it's not just family that matters. We know from our mentoring work that sometimes having a trusted adult, who perhaps isn't a relation, to talk to and spend time with, can really help children and young people when difficult times arise.

And finally, of course, children's friendships are vital. Interestingly, we found that seeing friends was much better for children than speaking to them either by phone or online. So helping your children to see their friends outside of school, if possible, will make a real difference.

BE ACTIVE

What we know

Around 7 per cent of children who exercise most days or every day have low well-being. For those who never or hardly ever do so, this rises to 18 per cent of children.

What you can do

Children need a range of opportunities to be active, both in- and outdoors. These can be as straightforward as walking, running, skipping, cycling or swimming, all of which are great at improving strength, balance, fitness and concentration.

Group sports are also good for enhancing self-confidence and cooperation and can help support new friendships outside of school. Local councils and libraries are usually the best places to begin to find out about what facilities and activities are available in your area.

Our work with young people in Cheshire uses sports to help them to develop trusting relationship with safe adults, often for the first time.

This again backs up what our research has told us about how developing children's well-being in one area can also help improve other areas of their lives.

BE CREATIVE AND PLAY

What we know

Only 7 per cent of children who learn new things for fun (like music, languages, art or drama) most days or every day have low well-being—this rises to 17 per cent of children who never or hardly ever do so.

What you can do

Children are naturally imaginative and creative. They can take an object and discover a hundred different uses for it, invent an entire character to be their imaginary friend or produce a masterpiece of modern art with just a crayon.

Sadly, as they get older, it's easy for children to lose these abilities.

This is why it's vital that they're encouraged to continue with some form of creative activity.

Magic shows, storytelling, collage making, poetry reading, and visiting some of the wonderful museums and galleries in the UK that offer free entry are all brilliant ways to get their creative juices flowing.

For children, it's almost impossible to separate creativity from play.

Happily, most children need little encouragement to do it because playing inside and out are essential to their emotional and physical development. National Playday have produced some top tips for parents (www.playday.org.uk/playday-events/top-tips/parents-families.aspx) to help encourage their children to play, and their verdict?

Turn off the TV and get outdoors, weather permitting of course!

LEARNING

What we know

Again, just 7 per cent of children who read for fun most days or every day have low well-being. This rises to 21 per cent for those who never or hardly ever do so.

What you can do

The children we spoke with were really clear that learning outside of school was just as important to them as learning at school. It was the sense of achievement that they felt from gaining new knowledge or skills that most mattered.

That's why it's crucial that we try to keep as many learning avenues open for our children as possible.

This could include simply passing on the skills we may have, such as cooking, carpentry, DIY, model making, sewing or photography.

The other way to encourage our children to learn is to model the attitudes towards learning that we'd like them to adopt. That's why one of the best ways to get your child to read for fun is to make sure that they see you regularly doing it as well.

Ultimately, children are natural learners; we just need to try and make their world as large as possible, by filling it with new experiences, cultures and ideas.

TAKE NOTICE

What we know

Just 5 per cent of children who notice and enjoy their surroundings most days or every day report low well-being. This rises to 33 per cent for children who never or hardly ever do so.

What you can do

We shouldn't underestimate how differently children see and interact with the world around them. Our rubbish is their treasure, a slug can be a friend, and stick them under a duvet with a torch and it's a whole new universe.

This also means that their surroundings have a real impact on their well-being. So while we'd all like to go on holiday more often, day trips to different types of places can help too. These could include city farms, local forests, the coast, even different parts of town can all help them to 'spread out' and enjoy a more varied environment.

From the report *How to support your child's well-being* produced by The Children's Society, www.childrenssociety.org.uk

Choice

Children's happiness with choice drops steadily between the ages of eight and 15, but then there is a marked rise at ages 16/17. This increase is greater than for any of the other aspects of life that are covered by The Good Childhood Index, suggesting that there is a mismatch between the amount of choice that children in their early teenage years have and how much they would like. Interviews with young people aged 14 and 15 about choice highlight a number of key themes for this age group, including the importance of having loving, supportive family relationships on the one hand, and being granted a reasonable level of choice/autonomy on the other.
The Good Childhood Report 2013: A summary of our findings, p. 4

Children's well-being is associated with the amount of autonomy that they perceive in their family relationships, regardless of the levels of family harmony and parental support, and vice versa.
The Good Childhood Report 2013: A summary of our findings, p. 4

Through local consultation work, The Children's Society learnt that children and young people need to be listened to, engaged and be able to make choices in their own lives and in things which affect them. This capacity to choose enables children to grow into adults who understand decision-making and consequences.

Listening to children and young people and involving them in decision-making is a cornerstone of the UN Convention on Rights of the Child. Seeing and hearing the world through the eyes of children gives us a unique perspective, which as adults we can no longer see or experience.

A group of children and young people were asked if they feel listened to by their church. The response of one 14-year-old boy was, 'I don't really know if they listen. I've never been asked.'

CORE SESSION FIVE: FAMILY WELL-BEING AND WHOLENESS

Personal reflection sheet

What did you learn from this session?

How will this affect the way you work with families?

What further items in this area would you like to follow up?

CORE SESSION FIVE: FAMILY WELL-BEING AND WHOLENESS

Portfolio checklist

Learning outcomes

- ✤ To gain a clearer understanding of the influence and impact of well-being on the life of families
- ✤ To develop thinking and inform future practice to ensure full participation by families in the life of the church

Write down what you have learnt in relation to these learning outcomes and how they might benefit your work with families.

To show that the learning outcomes have been achieved, your portfolio must include at least the following. *(Tick when you have included each one in the file.)*

☐ Personal reflection sheet

☐ Any notes taken during the session, with any additional ideas

☐ Any other responses/reflections you wish to include

The participant's involvement in a group for 'Core Session Five: Family well-being and wholeness' is confirmed

Signed (assessor)____________________________ Date __________

Any comments from assessor

Signed (candidate)____________________________ Date __________

CORE SESSION SIX

Faith in families

Aim

- To reflect on and understand the challenges and limitations that families may face in living out faith in the home
- To consider the ways in which the church can encourage, support and resource families in practical ways, and the resources available to do so

Learning outcomes

- To recognise the role of the church in supporting families to live out faith in the home in a way that is appropriate and accessible for families
- To recognise the different factors to be taken into account when working with families, such as age, experience, time and finance
- To equip leaders to help families create faith-filled homes

Materials needed

- A large drawing of a fruit bowl (page 70)—make this as large as possible to suit the number of group participants
- Paper or card copies of cherry and banana shapes (page 71), or sticky notes—one of each for each person
- Paper or card copies of apple shapes (page 71), or sticky notes—one of each for each person
- Copies of 'Houses outlines' handout sheet (page 72)
- Copies of 'Starting points for families' handout sheet (page 73)
- Copies of 'Living out faith in the home' handout sheet (page 74)
- Copies of 'Resources' handout sheet (page 76)
- Range of children's Bibles (optional)

Opening thought

The future of humanity passes by way of family.
Pope John Paul II, *Familiaris Consortio*, © Libreria Editrice Vaticana, 1981

Being a parent/carer is said to be one of the hardest jobs an adult will ever do. Whether someone agrees with this statement or not, the reality seems to be that being a parent/carer is a role that requires time, attention and a great deal of learning along the way.

Various studies and research have suggested that the parent/carer has the primary influence upon a child generally and that they also hold the primary responsibility for encouraging and supporting the development of faith. This is a significant responsibility alongside all the other roles. It can be a challenge for parents who have grown up with a knowledge and understanding of the Christian faith, and maybe even more so for those who have not grown up with this knowledge.

Starter

Icebreaker 

You will need

- ❋ A large drawing of a fruit bowl (page 70)—make this as large as possible to suit the number of group participants
- ❋ Paper or card copies of cherry and banana shapes (page 71), or sticky notes—one of each for each person

Set up the fruit bowl at the front of the room with the cherries and bananas alongside. Invite people to take a template of a cherry and banana. Discuss in twos.

- ✤ Do you feel the parents/carers you work with would agree with the opening statement and why?
- ✤ Think of one family you work with. What do you think the family would say is the main highlight of their life—the cherry on the cake, as it were? Write that on the cherry.
- ✤ What do you think they would say is the thing that is the most challenging in family life—the thing that drives them bananas? Write that on the banana.

Each person brings these to the front and places them on a large picture of a fruit bowl. Take time to have a look at them.

As a whole group, ask people to consider.

- ✤ Which one do you feel would be the highlight?
- ✤ Which one would be the most challenging?

Recognising the highlights and difficulties of family life is important when working with families. What challenges one may not challenge another. It is important to know the families individually.

Core teaching

Growing faith in the home 

You will need

- ❋ Copies of 'Houses outlines' handout sheet (page 72)
- ❋ Paper or card copies of apple shapes (page 71), or sticky notes—one of each for each person

The Good Childhood Report 2014 by The Children's Society found that 'family' was one of the top 10 factors expressed by children that contributed to their overall happiness and well-being. It also suggested that it was the strength of relationships that were significant rather than whether they were biologically related.

Within the breadth of family life, parents may be aware of the importance of meeting the physical needs but it is also vital to support the emotional, mental and spiritual aspects of life. The latter can be more challenging if the parents/carers don't feel they have the knowledge to do this.

Divide into groups of three or four. Give each group a copy of the handout with four outlines of houses of different shapes and sizes. Discuss as a group what the things are that help faith to grow in the home.

Write one in each of the different houses.

Living out faith in the home 

You will need

- ❋ Copies of 'Starting points for families' handout sheet (page 73)
- ❋ Copies of 'Living out faith in the home' handout sheet (page 74)

How can we encourage, support and equip families to live out faith in the home? Invite people to work in pairs and consider the following.

- ✤ Which of the 'starting points for families' do you feel would be of most encouragement to the families you work with? Write your thought on a paper or card apple (or sticky note).
- ✤ Which factor on the 'Living out faith in the home' handout sheet presents the greatest challenge for the families you work with?
- ✤ Which piece of encouragement or advice would you most like to pass on to them?

Write your thoughts on the other side of the apple (or on a sticky note).

Useful resources 

You will need

- ❋ Copies of 'Resources' handout sheet (page 76)
- ❋ Range of children's Bibles (optional)

If time allows, have a number of children's Bibles on display suitable for younger and older children and teenagers. Allow those at the session to browse to gain an idea of content and age suitability.

Biblical thought

But to all who did receive him, who believed in his name, he gave the right to become children of God.

John 1:12, ESV

How might this encourage your families that we are all invited to be the children of God? Regardless of age, background, knowledge or experience, we are all offered a place in God's family.

Talk about them [the commandments] wherever you are, sitting at home or walking in the street; talk about them from the time you get up in the morning to when you fall into bed at night.

Deuteronomy 6:7, *The Message*

Take time to think about what that might mean for the families they work with. How might they be encouraged to do this? Exploring faith is an ongoing journey throughout the everyday routines of life.

Reflection on learning

- What points most stood out for you from this session?
- What would be the three key points you would take away to use or share with the families you work with?

Worship

You will need

- Cherry and banana shapes from the starter activity

Each person comes and takes a cherry and a banana from the starter activity. Ask them to think of a family they know who springs to mind for what is written on the fruit, and to take a moment to pray for them, giving thanks and praying for their needs. They may like to take these away to continue to pray for them and other families.

Together, sing or listen to the song 'As for me and my house' by Jim Bailey, www.jimbailey.bandcamp.com/track/as-for-me-my-house.

Fruit bowl

Cherry, banana and apple shapes

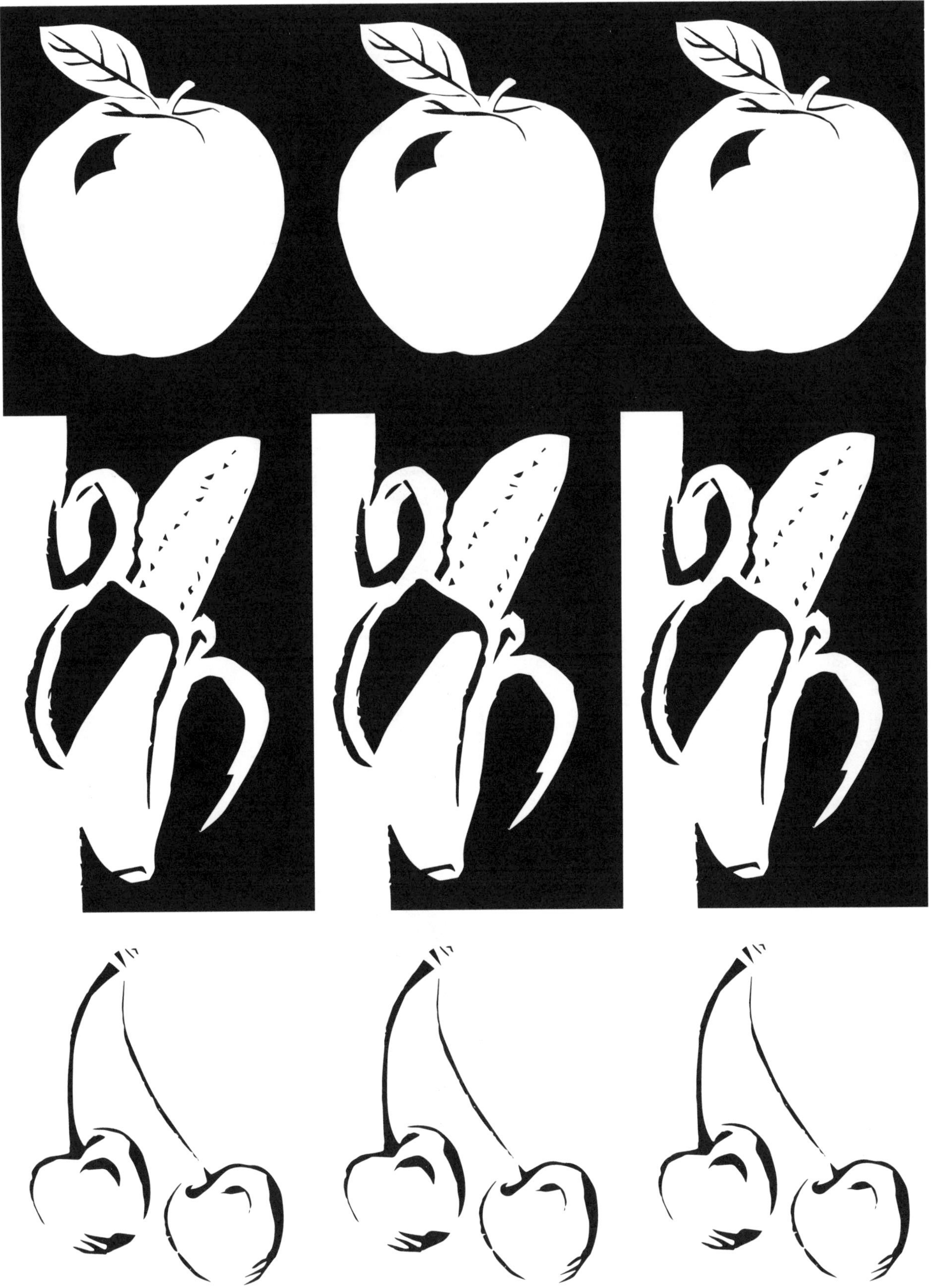

Houses outlines

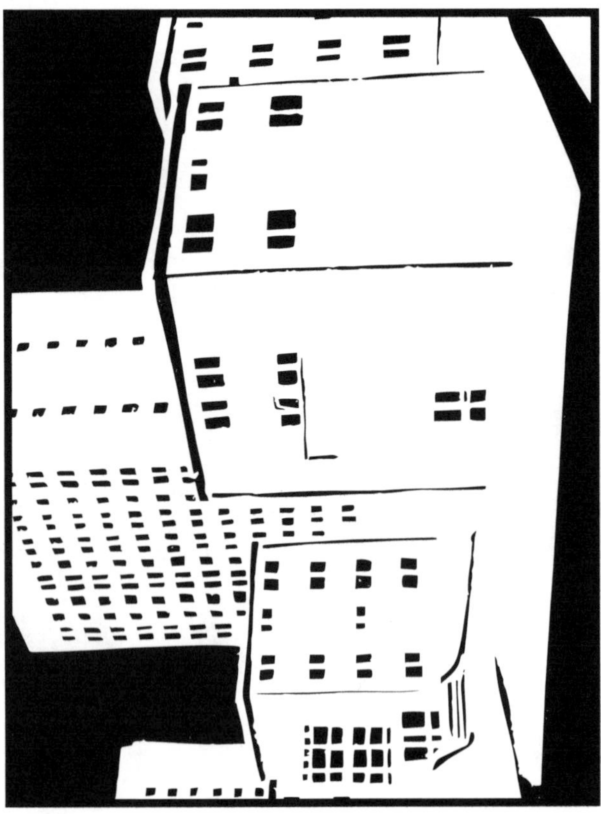

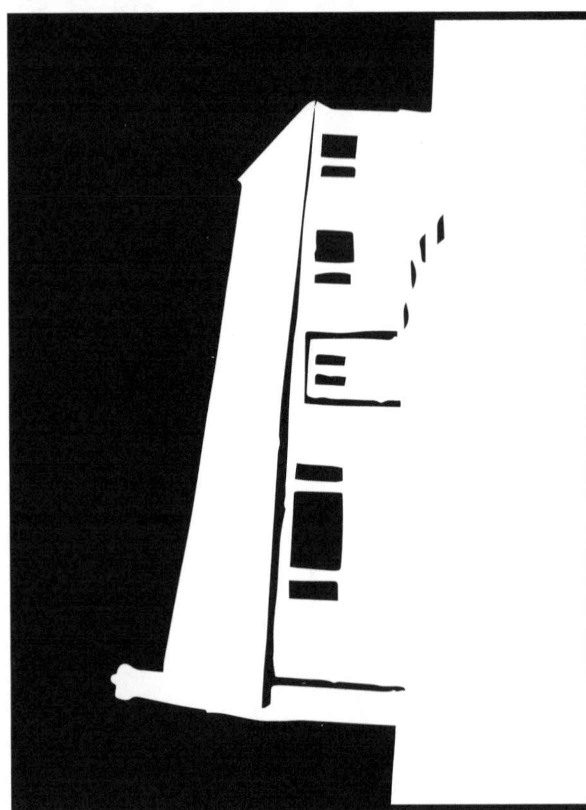

Starting points for families

Whatever a parent/carer's level of knowledge, there are some important points to recognise at the start.

Get started

It is never too late to start exploring, discussing and living out faith in the home.

Flexibility

There is no set or right way to live out faith in the home. Flexibility is a key aspect. What works for one family will not be right for another. It is important to work out what works best.

Build in

It does not necessarily require families to add pressure to their already busy lives by creating numerous additional hours of activities every week. It is possible to build faith into the everyday activities they already do.

Learn together

Adults do not have to know all the answers. It is more about being on a journey together as a family. People may all be at different stages but enjoy the opportunity to explore, discuss and enjoy the journey by learning about faith together.

No judgement!

It is not about measuring levels of faith and does not involve success and failure. Faith is an ongoing learning experience throughout life.

Include others

Faith in the home is not necessarily restricted to those living under the same roof but can include the extended family, friends and the wider church. For those in a church setting, inviting those who are single, divorced or widowed offers richness and offers important relationships to be established. This may be even more beneficial if a family does not live near to or see their relatives.

Have fun!

Whatever their preference and learning styles, one of the key aspects is enjoyment! It may take a while but it is worth taking the time to find out what works best for a family, taking into consideration age, time and budget available and being willing to be flexible and adapt as the seasons of family life change.

Living out faith in the home

Take into account the following factors when offering support and resources to families.

Appropriate language and content when selecting Bible stories

There is a range of Bibles available for children and young adults. It is helpful if families can be given guidance as to what is appropriate to different age groups (see 'Resources' handout, p. 76, for details).

Existing experience/knowledge of faith

The perception of exploring faith at home may centre around reading the Bible together for some families. For many, though, this may not be easy if they have never done this previously. Alternative ways to explore faith through activities and discussions may be more helpful.

Time and financial constraints

For some families there may be limitations on the time and budget available.

Exploring faith within the existing patterns and routines of family life is important to make it feel achievable. Examples may include praying before meals or bed, reading a Bible story before bed or after a family meal.

A walk to school with younger children can open up conversations about creation, for example. For older children that time might be an opportunity to talk about relationships if issues are raised at school. How does that connect with faith and what can we learn from the Bible about relationships with others?

For those with teenagers, the 'taxi service' facility offered by parents/carers can provide a valuable time for talking about life issues and the connection with faith.

Appropriate length of time for attention spans

Consider different means of exploring faith that will keep people's attention.

Example: An active eleven-year-old boy was struggling to concentrate and participate in a Bible study with his family. Although using a children's Bible, he was more interested in creating his own entertainment. All seemed lost when dad also left the room. However, a few minutes later he returned with a blindfold and a plate of food hidden under a cloth. In turn each person had to be blindfolded, taste a piece of food, say what it was and where in a Bible story it could be found.

Within seconds all five people, adults and children, were engaged.

All had Bible knowledge, so the activity was an appropriate level. This example can be used to highlight the general point of using the best means to connect at any level.

Ages of children in the family

Make sure the Bible stories or the activities offered are suitable for the ages of the children. Be open to discussing faith with children of all ages. Start from where they are at.

Example: A dad shared some thoughts about how he has chatted about faith with his son through the years. He felt the key was spending time to get to know his son, being ready and willing to discuss anything and answer questions when possible and to be an example of how God was working in his life today through the difficulties and the successes.

'As my son (now 16) has grown, the nature of these times has changed but it has always involved having time together. Maybe it was doing DIY together, giving him the opportunity to make holes in walls, or working in the garden, which he loves, when suddenly out of the blue there was a deep question. I remember thinking, "It's time to stop, listen and take time to respond—don't just get on with the next thing on the to-do list or give a quick answer."'

Learning styles of family members

Some may prefer a study-based approach while others may prefer an activity or something discussion-based. Varying the styles will meet these needs and offer a 'freshness' of approach, particularly as ages and stages alter. Options are using craft, cookery or construction to link into the theme of the Bible story/faith concept, and watching films by way of opening up discussion. This may be particularly appropriate for families who have not been familiar with talking about faith together, or with older children who are no longer around for family meals.

Resources

Websites and resources are subject to frequent change. At the time of going to press the following information is correct. There will be others in addition to these.

Websites

Faith in Homes: www.faithinhomes.org.uk
Flame Creative Ministries: www.flamecreativekids.blogspot.co.uk
Here to stay: www.here2stay.org.au
Scripture Union: www.scriptureunion.org.uk/Families/871.id
Commonsense Media: www.commonsensemedia.org
Whatisorange.org: whatisorange.org/252basics
The Children's Society: www.childrenssociety.org.uk

Pinterest pages

www.pinterest.com/revmaryhawes/faith-in-the-home/
www.pinterest.com/revmaryhawes/playing-the-faith/
www.pinterest.com/revmaryhawes/early-years-websites-and-resources/
www.uk.pinterest.com/MethodistCYF/

Children's Bibles

General children's Bibles and storybooks: www.eden.co.uk/childrens-bible
Pinterest: www.pinterest.com/revmaryhawes/children-s-bibles-and-bible-story-books
Guidance for choosing Bibles: www.thegoodbook.co.uk/choosing-a-childrens-bible

Bibliography

Lynn Alexander, *Children, Families and God*, Evangelista Media, 2012
Michael and Michelle Anthony, *A Theology of Family Ministries*, Broadman & Holman, 2011
Vern Bengtson, Norella Putney and Susan Harris, *Families and Faith*, Oxford University Press, 2013
Marcia Bunge, *The Child in the Bible*, Eerdmans, 2008
Kenneth Hanson and Douglas Oakman, *Palestine in the time of Jesus*, Fortress Press, 2008
William Strange, *Children in the Early Church*, Wipf & Stock, 2004
James M. White, David M. Klein and Todd F. Martin, *Family Theories*, Sage Publications, 2014
Diana Garland, *Family Ministry: A comprehensive guide*, IVP, 2012

Personal reflection sheet

What did you learn from this session?

How will this affect the way you work with families?

What further items in this area would you like to follow up?

CORE SESSION SIX: FAITH IN FAMILIES

Portfolio checklist

Learning outcomes

- ✤ To recognise the role of the church in supporting families to live out faith in the home in a way that is appropriate and accessible for families
- ✤ To recognise the different factors to be taken into account when working with families, such as age, experience, time and finance
- ✤ To equip leaders to help families create faith-filled homes

Choose two of these learning outcomes. Write down what you have learnt in relation to these and how they might benefit your work with families.

To show that the learning outcomes have been achieved, your portfolio must include at least the following. *(Tick when you have included each one in the file.)*

☐ Personal reflection sheet

☐ Any notes taken during the session, with any additional ideas

☐ Any other responses/reflections you wish to include

The participant's involvement in a group for 'Core Session Six: Faith in families' is confirmed

Signed (assessor)______________________________ Date __________

Any comments from assessor

Signed (candidate)______________________________ Date __________

Notes

Notes